Weather Data
How To Find It and
How To Process It

by D. James Benton

software available free online

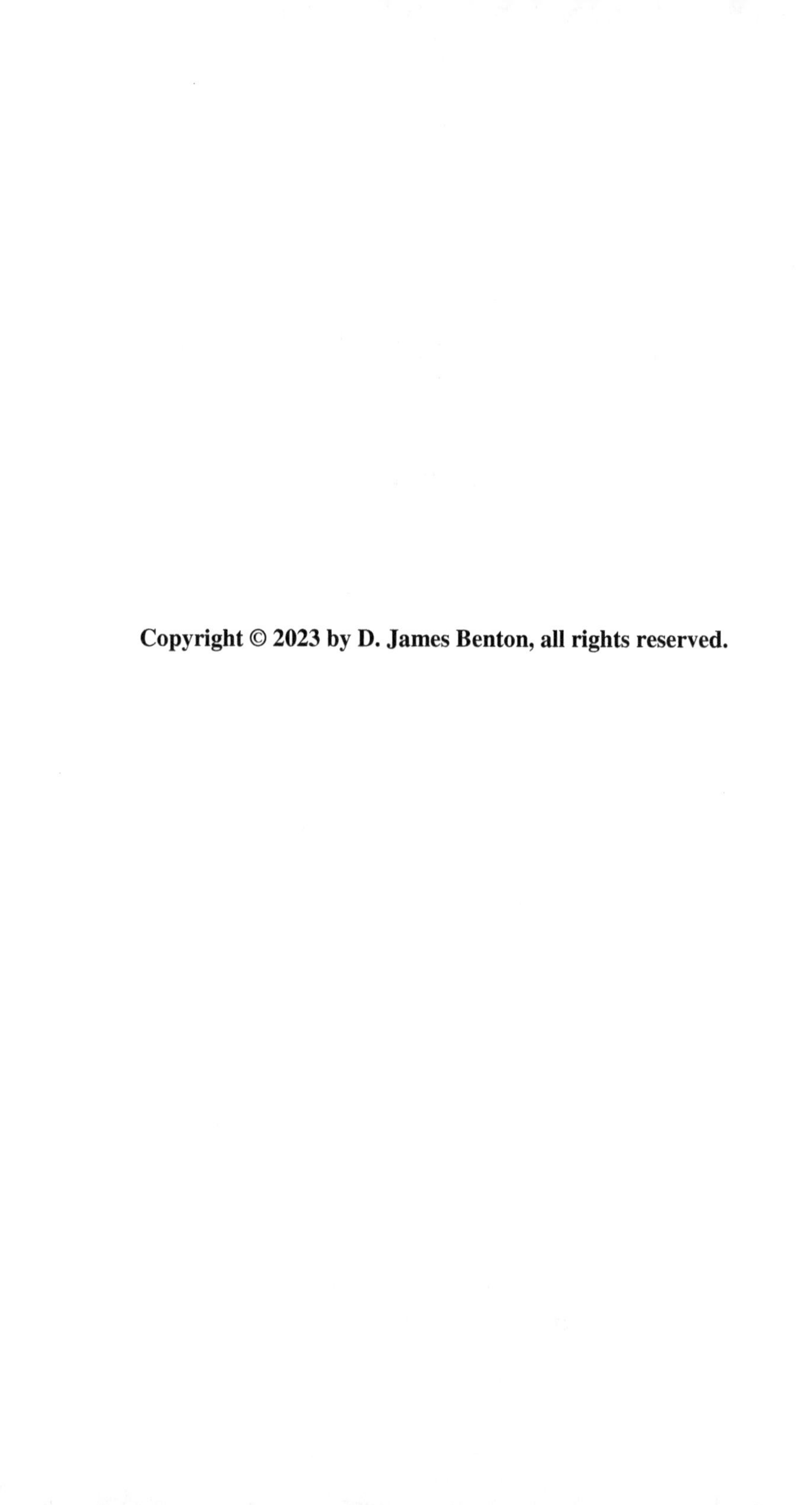

Preface

In this text we discuss bulk weather data, not yesterday's high or tomorrow's chances for rain. Archived data for thousands of meteorological stations over decades of record are available free at several locations on the Web. We will discuss these collections, what they contain, and how to access them. We will only discuss *raw* meteorological data, not *cooked* data, which has been pre-processed. We will not push any particular climate narrative; rather, we will examine the data and let it speak for itself.

All of the examples contained in this book,
(as well as a lot of free programs) are available at...
https://www.dudleybenton.altervista.org/software/index.html

Figure 1. Mollweide Projection Showing Countries

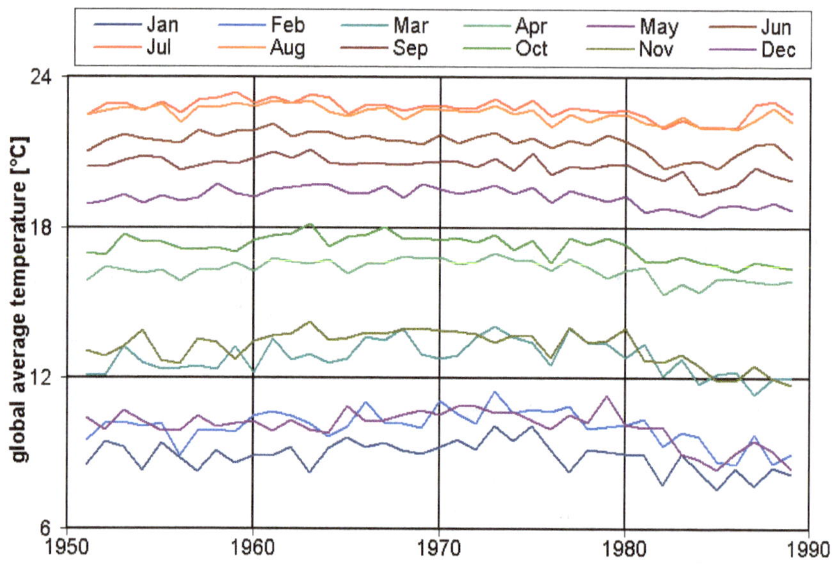

Figure 2. Global Average Temperature by Month Based on GHCN

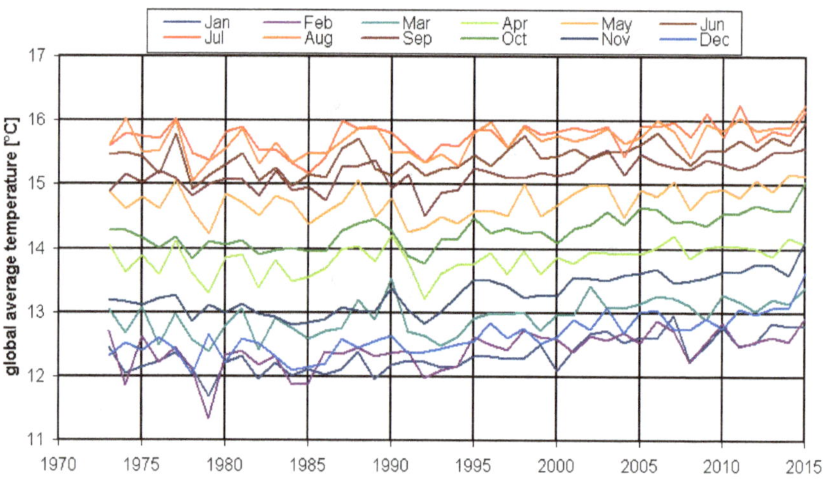

Figure 3. Global Average Temperature by Month Based on GSOD

The results in both of these figures are calculated using area-weighted averages. The areas are based on triangular grids covering the globe using the meteorological station locations as vertices. As we discuss in this text, the size and coverage of the data set can significantly impact the results—even when using the same algorithm.

Table of Contents   Page

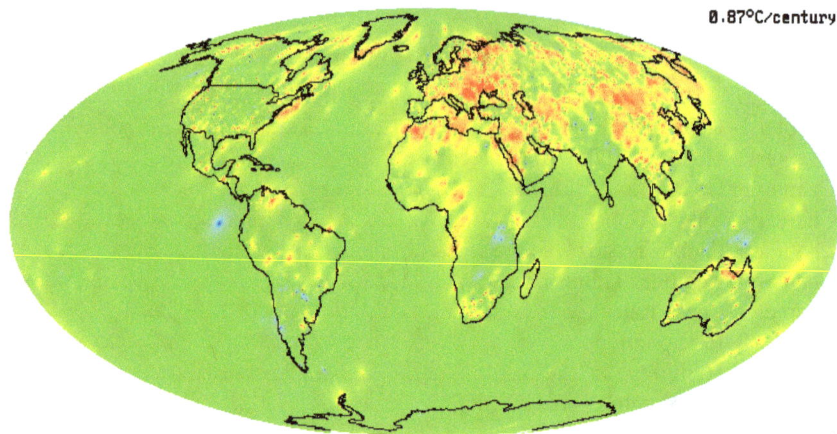

Figure 4. Fifty-Year Temperature Trend (GSOD)

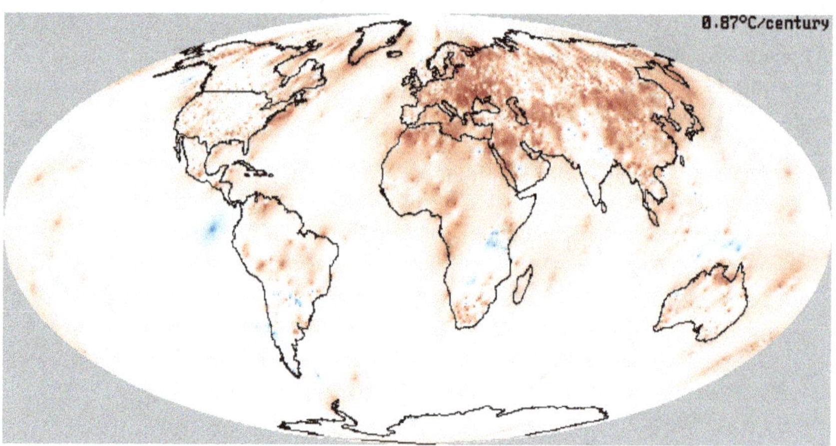

Figure 5. Same Information with Different Palette

  These two figures illustrate a psychological effect in contemporary Western Society. Information is often presented in such a way as to produce a desired response. In the case of climate data, the desired response is usually panic. Sadly, panic is not conducive to making wise decisions.

Chapter 1. GHCN/NDP-041 Collection

I have been studying the Earth's climate since 1980, when I began work at the Tennessee Valley Authority's Engineering Laboratory. Our Team had many projects that included weather data. This was also when climate change was a newly rising concern. As many of our analyses depended on weather data—both past (known) conditions and also future (forecast) conditions. Over the past 43 years, I have processed a lot of this data and developed many software tools to facilitate its analysis. In the early days, this data came in the form of hourly values stored on reel-to-reel magnetic tape. I still have some of this data, only now stored in Excel™ spreadsheets. TVA maintains its own meteorological stations, as did the National Weather Service (NWS).

Much data from many stations (mostly in the form of daily summaries) may be found on the Web. Hourly data is more difficult to find but we will discuss this later. These data have been gathered into several collections, going back as far as 1697. One such example is shown below:

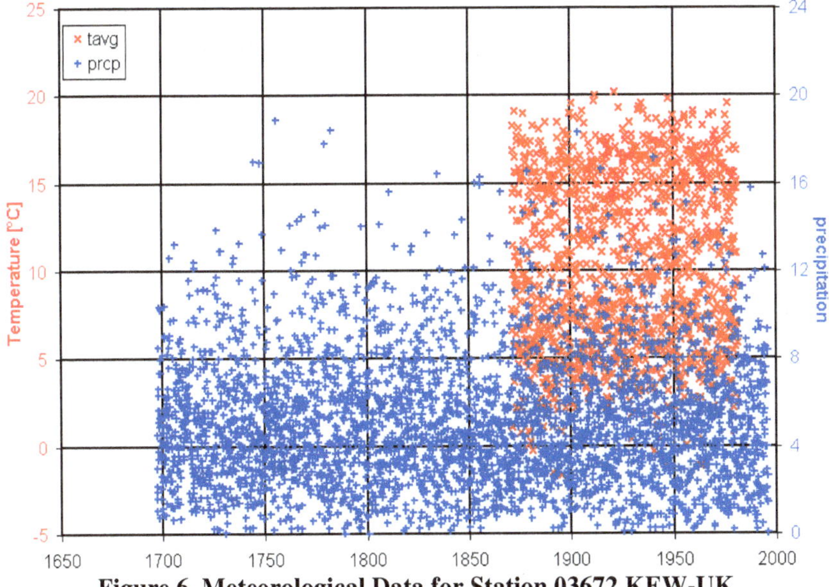

Figure 6. Meteorological Data for Station 03672 KEW-UK

Obviously, these data were collected "by hand" and written down on paper, only later transferred to digital format and archived. This data set illustrates a common challenge: missing data, which is more often the case with older data. If you are studying long-range patterns or trends, older data is important and so you will have to deal with missing data. This data set is part of the Global Historical Climatology Network (GHCN) and may be found at the National Centers for Environmental Information (NCEI) website:

https://www.ncei.noaa.gov/

maintained by the National Oceanographic and Atmospheric Administration (NOAA). Additional data may be found at the National Climate Data Center (NCDC) website:

https://www.ncdc.noaa.gov/

also maintained by NOAA. You can download all of GHCN data for free at the website above. The files are compressed using gzip (a UNIX utility) and gathered into "tar balls" (a UNIX multi-file archive format). These may be accessed on UNIX or LINUX using the readily available tools. There are several tools available for Windows™ to access these files, including WinZip™. You can also read the data without manually un-tarring and un-gzipping, using special software, as described in Appendix E. GHCN stations are shown below:

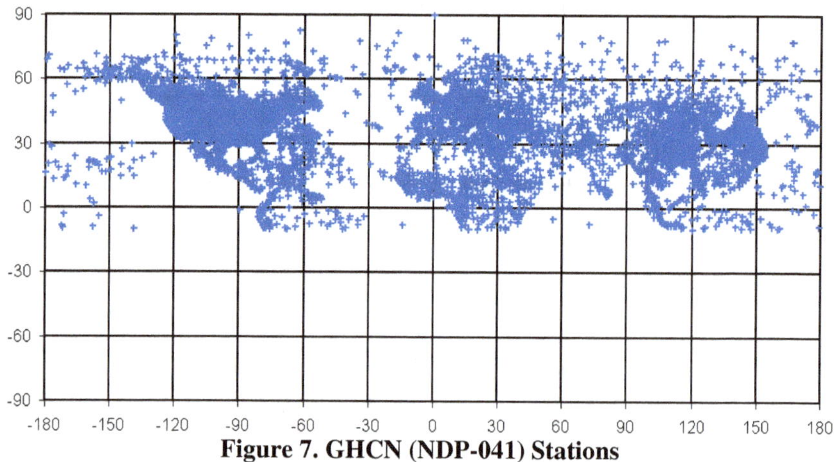

Figure 7. GHCN (NDP-041) Stations

If you are studying global meteorology, the figure above reveals a big problem: there is no data below -10° latitude or roughly 44% of the Earth's surface. If you are focusing on North America or Europe or Asia, this data set would be of considerable interest, as it includes some very old years. This same database has also appeared under the designation NDP-041. The specific format of the data files has also changed somewhat over the past few decades.

This next figure shows the number of stations in this data set reporting temperatures for each month and year:

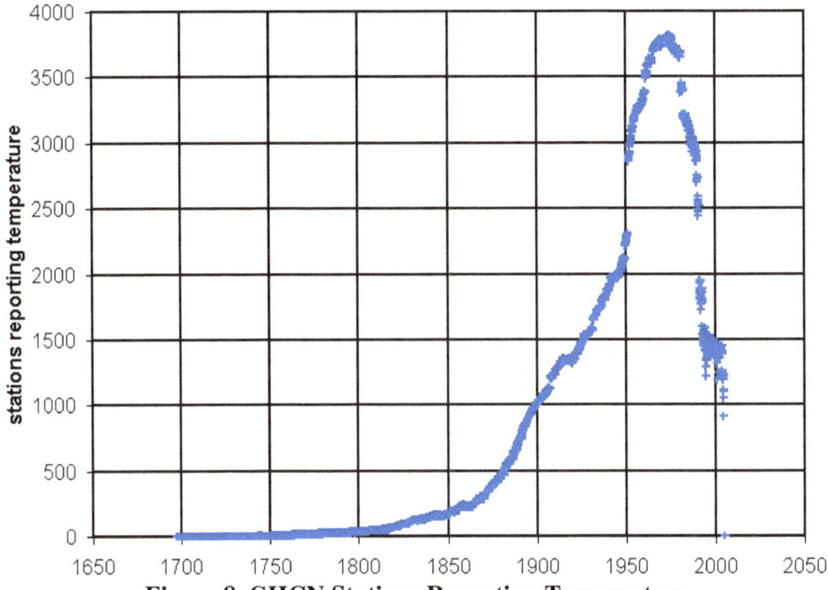

Figure 8. GHCN Stations Reporting Temperature

So, not only does this data set lack stations below -10° latitude, but it also only contains a substantial number of stations reporting temperature for 1950 through 1989. Still, there are some very old data and if your interest falls within these limitations, this data set can be useful. This data set contains monthly minimum, maximum, and average temperature, along with monthly precipitation, but no daily data, which is also a limitation.

Before we leave this data set to consider others, let us first consider temperature maps, including global ones. Maps of temperature appear each evening on the news but where do these come from, as only point measurements are available. The short answer: some sort of interpolation or modeling. Methods for interpolation abound and many are used to create temperature maps. No method is without bias, as all depend on various assumptions, which may or may not be accurate. Some algorithms tend to weight closely-packed (spatially near) data more heavily, while others tend to smooth out the "lumps" more evenly. Sadly, in today's political climate, an algorithm that tends to skew data toward a preferred narrative may be selected over one that lacks such a preferential view of the data.

The station locations shown in the preceding figure shows considerable spatial variability: many stations are closely packed in some areas and sparsely spread out in other areas. The computational journey between specific data points and a smooth mapping over the entire surface of the Earth can be a tortuous one, fraught with many pitfalls. We will discuss this process at some length in subsequent chapters. One such mapping using the GHCN data for December 1898 is shown below:

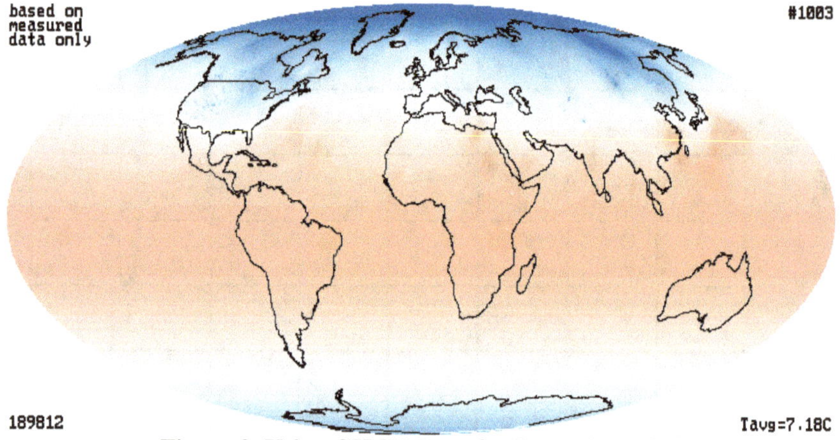

Figure 9. Using GHCN Data for December 1898

The selection of colors can also affect the narrative. Bold, bright or deep reds can communicate pending disaster and encourage fear. The same information in different colors is shown in this next figure:

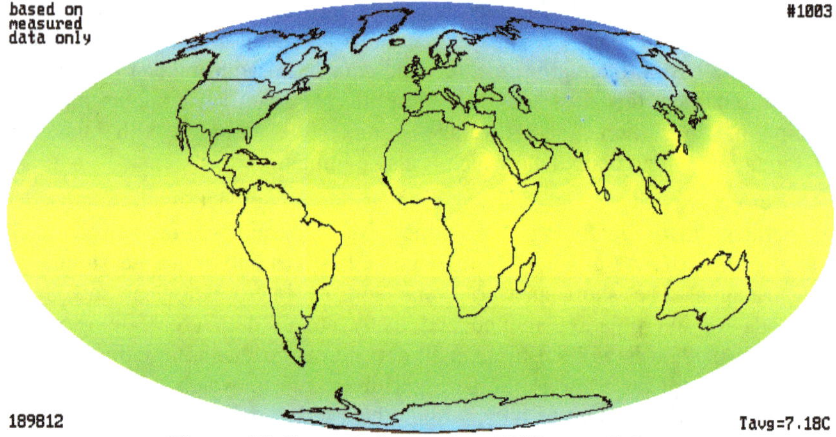

Figure 10. Same Information, Different Colors

The global average temperature by month for 1951 through 1989 using this database is shown at the top of page i. The method of calculation will be discussed in Chapter 2.

<u>Extracting the GHCN Data</u>

The GHCN/NDP-041 data set comes in a UNIX tarball that can be opened in WinZip to reveal the contents:

Name	Type	Modified	Size	Ratio	Packed
read.data.f	F File	6/12/2002 5:13 PM	10,988	67%	3,594
read.inv.f	F File	6/12/2002 5:13 PM	2,902	56%	1,291
readme.precip.v2	V2 File	11/30/1999 11:13 PM	5,538	60%	2,195
readme.txt	Readme Do...	11/30/1999 11:13 PM	4,022	55%	1,824
readrain2.f	F File	8/2/2000 12:44 PM	11,105	65%	3,846
v2.max	MAX File	12/24/2004 3:13 AM	21,927,444	74%	5,678,833
v2.max.failed.qc	QC File	12/24/2004 3:13 AM	89,559	78%	19,430
v2.max_adj	MAX_ADJ File	12/24/2004 3:13 AM	17,673,887	74%	4,635,278
v2.mean	MEAN File	12/24/2004 3:13 AM	44,932,811	77%	10,332,833
v2.mean.failed.qc	QC File	12/24/2004 3:13 AM	551,097	81%	103,093
v2.mean_adj	MEAN_ADJ ...	12/24/2004 3:13 AM	32,115,699	75%	8,037,065
v2.min	MIN File	12/24/2004 3:13 AM	22,018,073	74%	5,621,920
v2.min.failed.qc	QC File	12/24/2004 3:13 AM	166,293	80%	33,403
v2.min_adj	MIN_ADJ File	12/24/2004 3:13 AM	17,769,752	74%	4,594,080
v2.prcp	PRCP File	12/24/2004 3:13 AM	81,610,837	70%	24,510,663
v2.prcp.failed.qc	QC File	12/24/2004 3:13 AM	654,480	78%	144,460
v2.prcp.failed.qc_pre1997	QC_PRE1997...	6/19/2002 12:19 PM	627,642	78%	138,773
v2.prcp_adj	PRCP_ADJ File	12/24/2004 3:13 AM	16,970,646	69%	5,330,333

Selected 0 files, 0 bytes — Total 18 files, 251,116KB

Figure 11. Contents of GHCN/NDP-041 Tarball

Information about the collection may be found in readme.txt. Three FORTRAN 77 source files (*.f) are included to facilitate reading the data. An abbreviated excerpt from read.inf.f appears below:

```
      program read_inv
      character name*30,grveg*16,pop*1,topo*2,stveg*2
      character stloc*2,airstn*1
      open(unit=1,file='v2.inv')
100   read(1,102,end=200)ic,iwmo,imod,name,rlat,
     +rlong,ielevs,ielevg,pop,ipop,topo,stveg,
     +stloc,iloc,airstn,itowndis,grveg
102   format(i3.3,i5.5,i3.3,1x,a30,1x,f6.2,1x,f7.2,
     +1x,i4,1x,i4,a1,i5,3(a2),i2,a1,i2,a16)
      go to 100
200   continue
      end
```

A sample of the contents of v2.mean is shown below:

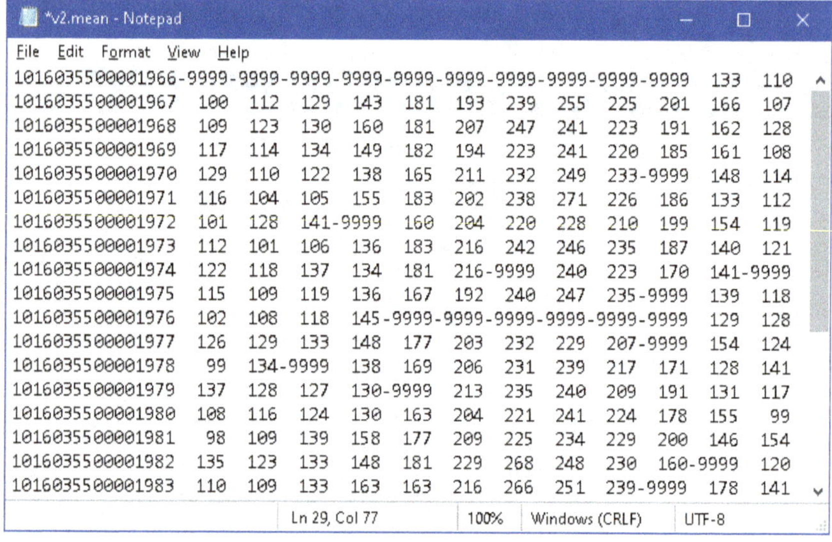

```
*v2.mean - Notepad
File  Edit  Format  View  Help
10160355000001966-9999-9999-9999-9999-9999-9999-9999-9999-9999-9999   133   110
10160355000001967   100   112   129   143   181   193   239   255   225   201   166   107
10160355000001968   109   123   130   160   181   207   247   241   223   191   162   128
10160355000001969   117   114   134   149   182   194   223   241   220   185   161   108
10160355000001970   129   110   122   138   165   211   232   249   233-9999   148   114
10160355000001971   116   104   105   155   183   202   238   271   226   186   133   112
10160355000001972   101   128   141-9999   160   204   220   228   210   199   154   119
10160355000001973   112   101   106   136   183   216   242   246   235   187   140   121
10160355000001974   122   118   137   134   181   216-9999   240   223   170   141-9999
10160355000001975   115   109   119   136   167   192   240   247   235-9999   139   118
10160355000001976   102   108   118   145-9999-9999-9999-9999-9999-9999   129   128
10160355000001977   126   129   133   148   177   203   232   229   207-9999   154   124
10160355000001978    99   134-9999   138   169   206   231   239   217   171   128   141
10160355000001979   137   128   127   130-9999   213   235   240   209   191   131   117
10160355000001980   108   116   124   130   163   204   221   241   224   178   155    99
10160355000001981    98   109   139   158   177   209   225   234   229   200   146   154
10160355000001982   135   123   133   148   181   229   268   248   230   160-9999   120
10160355000001983   110   109   133   163   163   216   266   251   239-9999   178   141

Ln 29, Col 77              100%    Windows (CRLF)    UTF-8
```

Figure 12. Contents of vw.mean

The minimum, maximum, and average (mean) temperatures can be found in groups of three separate files. As described in readme.txt, also included are data that failed the quality check (*.failed.qc). This collection also includes data that has been "adjusted to account for various non-climatic inhomogeneities". It is quite unusual to have the "before" and "after" values—something that makes this data set and the Team that created it very special. Another detail that this collection provides is also quite interesting: site descriptions, including:

ANTARCTICA	HIGHLAND SHRUB	TROP. MONTANE
BOGS, BOG WOODS	HOT DESERT	TROP. SAVANNA
COASTAL EDGES	ICE	TROP. SEASONAL
COLD IRRIGATED	LOW SCRUB	TROPICAL DRY FOR
COOL CONIFER	MAIN TAIGA	TUNDRA
COOL CROPS	MARSH, SWAMP	WARM CONIFER
COOL DESERT	MED. GRAZING	WARM CROPS
COOL FIELD/WOODS	NORTH. TAIGA	WARM DECIDUOUS
COOL FOR./FIELD	PADDYLANDS	WARM FIELD WOODS
COOL GRASS/SHRUB	POLAR DESERT	WARM FOR./FIELD
COOL IRRIGATED	SAND DESERT	WARM GRASS/SHRUB
COOL MIXED	SEMIARID WOODS	WARM IRRIGATED
E. SOUTH. TAIGA	SIBERIAN PARKS	WARM MIXED
EQ. EVERGREEN	SOUTH. TAIGA	WATER
HEATHS, MOORS	SUCCULENT THORNS	WOODED TUNDRA

Data Description

As mentioned previously for the GHCN collection, bulk meteorological data most often contain daily values of minimum, maximum, and/or average temperatures. These may be in °C or °F, a cursory inspection should indicate which. Furthermore, these are often be stored as integer values multiplied by ten (i.e., 10x), eliminating the decimal point. This practice serves to reduce file size. Some collections store data in binary rather than text (i.e., ASCII). Temperatures x10 become short (2-byte) signed integers, occupying even less space.

Little Endian vs. Big Endean

If the data are stored in binary format, beware that byte order is not the same on all machines. If the hardware is built so that the lowest (least significant) byte of a multi-byte value is stored first (at the lowest memory address), then the hardware is said to be "little-endian". Machines such as the Intel/AMD x86 and x64, Digital VAX and Alpha are little-endian. If the hardware is built so that the highest (most significant) byte of a multi-byte value is stored first (at the lowest memory address), then the hardware is said to be "big-endian". Machines such as IBM mainframes, Motorola, Sun SPARC, PowerPC, and most RISC machines are big-endian. Note that many large data collection efforts undertaken by the U.S. Government began before the proliferation of PCs and originated in the early days of the Web when most servers were UNIX machines. If the data appear quite strange, it may be due to hardware differences on which the collections were stored. Advice related to this issue specifically for your platform can readily be found on the Web.

Frequency of Data Collection

Minimum, maximum, and average data—especially from long past—is derived from multiple readings, most often 8 or 24 per day, not every 3 milliseconds. Even if such capability (rapid data collection) is readily available today, it is rarely used to compile bulk meteorological data, as each of these sets extends across years when this was not the case. Continuing onward, accumulating new data after old, requires some level of consistency; otherwise, the data are not compatible.

Data Quality

Some data sets include one or more indicators of data quality, often as bit flags. This information can be helpful when additional scrutiny is indicated. Examples of when this would be the case include: localized weather disasters, observed anomalies, rare conditions, and even contractual acceptance testing. I have been embroiled in several arguments when fractions of a degree mean the difference between passing and failing or lawsuits.

Pressure Data

Barometric pressure is an important meteorological quantity. It is most often reported in millibar (mb). A millibar is one-thousandths of a bar or 100 Pa

7

(pascal). A pascal is one newton per square meter. Standard atmosphere is 1013.25 mb or 101.325 kPa (kilopascal) or 14.696 psia (pounds per square inch absolute). Thus you will often see values rolling between 985 and 1045, as this is the typical range over the Earth. Beware that meteorological may be reported in station pressure (STP) at the station elevation and/or adjusted to sea level (SLP). In the event that it isn't clear which one is being reported, check the long-range average. If the average is noticeably less than 1013, this is probably local pressure.

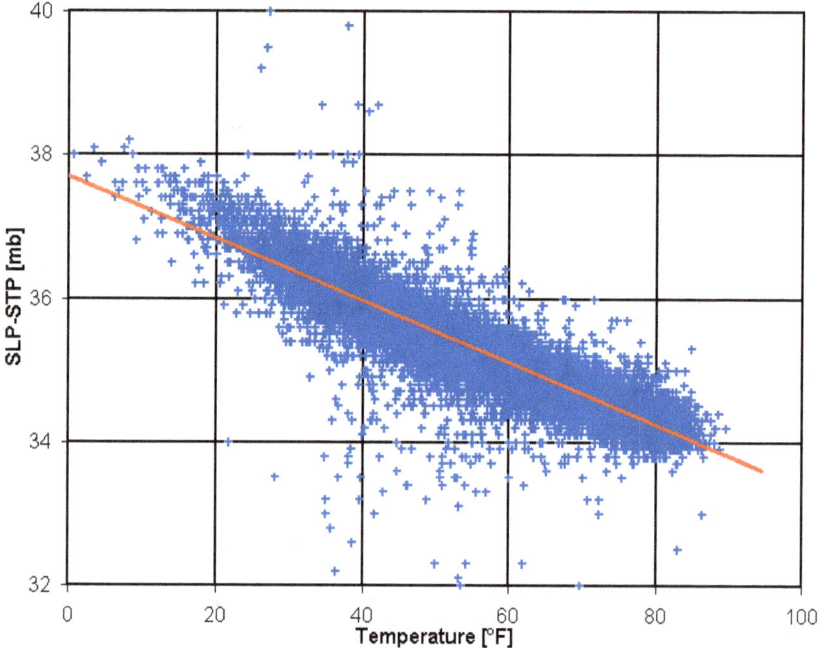

Figure 13. SLP-STP for Station 723260-13891

The station elevation should be available. Also beware that the "adjustment" from station to sea level pressure can vary. A quick perusal of the Web may not reveal this important detail. The "adjustment" might be a constant (typical?) value for a particular station in a particular data set or it might be one of several calculations. The "adjustment" might be the current (local) air density times the station elevation or it might be the standard density (which also varies, depending on which source you get this from) times the station elevation or it could be a more elaborate calculation. Several formulas can be found on the Web. The relative prominence of these nor the certainty of the blogger should be taken as proof that the algorithm presented was used for the station of interest in the data set you are using. The preceding figure shows 76 years for one station:

This meteorological station is at the McGhee-Tyson Airport, elevation 296 meters above MSL (mean sea level). The scatter shows that no simple "adjustment" was used for this station. The "adjustment" used at this station in this data set clearly includes more than one term (in addition to current temperature). If we include local pressure (i.e., two-terms) in the correction, the scatter is similar. If we include current moisture (i.e., three-terms) in the correction, the scatter persists. It is difficult to determine from the data alone what calculation was used to "adjust" the data, which may have changed over time, resulting in some or even most of the scatter.

Mixed Units

This figure and data set illustrate another important detail: mixed units. Do not presume that all the quantities in any particular database will be consistently SI or English units. Both may be present. I have seen data sets that switch from °F to °C at some year or even half-way through a year. This discontinuity would jump out of a plot but other shifts may not, so be careful. Use common sense and look at a range of data.

Precipitation

While temperatures may be reported in °F or more often °C, precipitation is most often reported in inches x100 (or hundredths of an inch to eliminate a decimal point and reduce file size). Again, check for mixed SI and English units in your database. Snowfall is most often reported in the same units as (wet) precipitation and is generally "melted" snow time some arbitrary "packing" factor chosen by whoever is doing this. Values of snowfall that appear in bulk meteorological databases are almost never literally measured. As with the "adjustment" from STP to SLP, a quick perusal of the Web might not reveal the variety of means used to enter snowfall. Someone who is adamant that the snow depth to data reporting transformation is precise and consistent may be familiar with a very limited data set, such at the one they have used in Germany for the past 1200 years.

Also beware that rain gauge data may be a rough indicator of precipitation but when scrutinized, is a joke. Do you seriously believe the little plastic tube shown in the following picture collects a representative sample of what's falling from the sky? If you really care about actual average rainfall, at least use a plastic kiddy pool if not an olympic-sized swimming pool to collect it. When I worked at TVA, we would "adjust" the reported rainfall each month to match the "measured" amount actually collected in the many dams throughout the region and the adjustments were not trivial.

Figure 14. Rain Gauge

NOAA's Atmospheric Turbulence Lab in Oak Ridge, Tennessee routinely uses plastic kiddy pools to collect samples.

Figure 15. Plastic Kiddy Pool

Chapter 2. USHCN/NDP-070 Collection

In your search for bulk meteorological data you will encounter many acronyms. The full name of the second collection we will examine is: USHCN ORNL/CDIAC-118 NDP-070 or the United States Historical Climatology Network, Oak Ridge National Laboratory, Carbon Dioxide Information Analysis Center, Numeric Data Package. As per the accompanying documentation, this collection includes: corrections for data inhomogeneities and nonclimatic influences as well as quality assurance checks and adjustments. This—like the previous collection—is the result of much work by many scientists over decades. The data includes: daily temperature, precipitation, and snow accumulation. The CDIAC website is listed below:

https://data.ess-dive.lbl.gov/portals/CDIAC

The NDP-070 collection can be found there. This collection includes data from 1062 stations shown in this first figure:

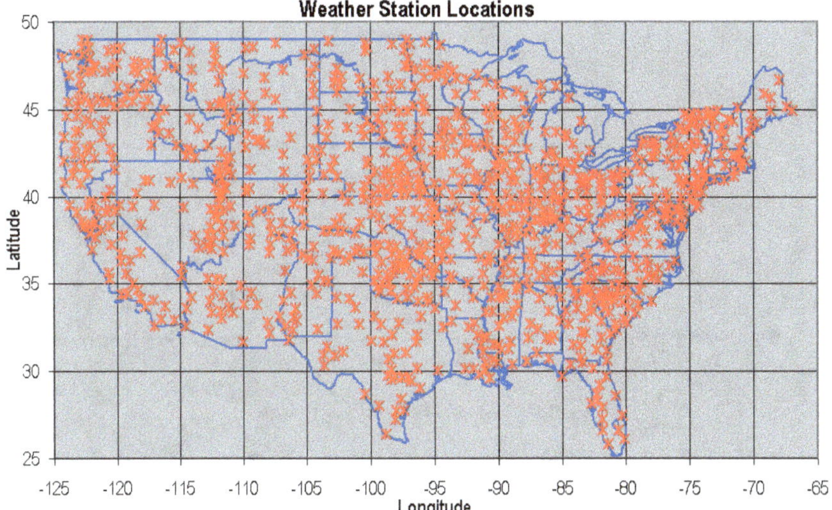

Figure 16. NDP-070 Stations

While this collection is limited to stations within the 48 contiguous (US) states, it does contain some interesting details and long continuous records. To give you an idea of how much information this is, the compressed repository is 150MB and 29,249,860 daily records extending from 1872 through 2002. This collection will also serve to illustrate how the data can be processed and analyzed. The data include: minimum, maximum, and average daily temperature plus precipitation, snow fall, and snow depth. Over the lifetime of this collection the organization of the archive has changed. At one time the data were stored by station. At some time later the data were stored by type (i.e., temperature in one file and precipitation in another). I would prefer to have this (and all such) data organized by station or by year but this can easily be accomplished with a little code.

Coverage

The first detail after station locations that we will consider is coverage; that is, completeness by station and year. This is shown for this collection in the figure below:

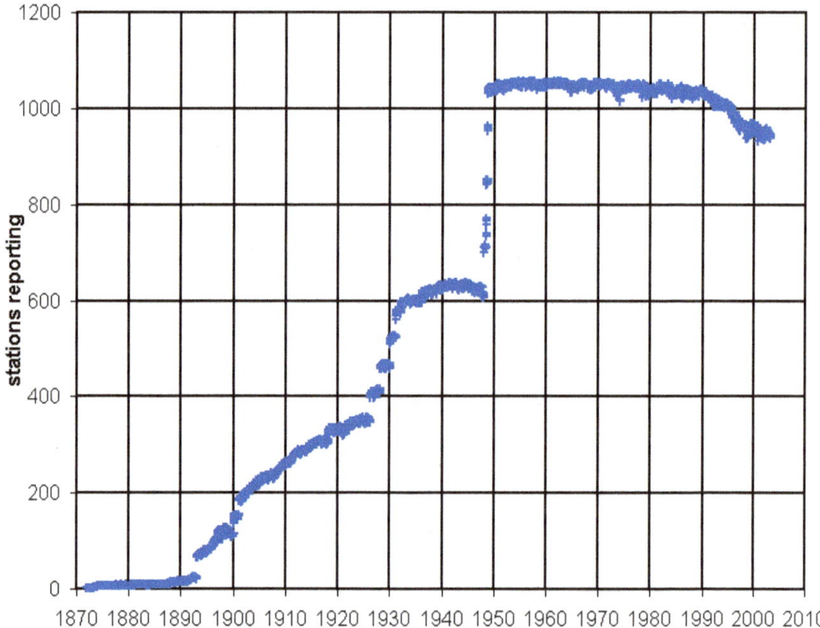

Figure 17. NDP-070 Coverage

From this we see that the most extensive coverage for this collection extends from about 1949 through 2002 with approximately half the total number of stations for 1931 through 1948. This illustrates a common challenge with this type of data: no collection is perfect or complete. In every study, the climate scientist must decide not only how to process the available data but also how to handle the data that isn't available.

Creating a Temperature Map

Perhaps the first step in processing this type of data is creating a temperature map. To illustrate this, we select one day with most of the stations reporting that also exhibits considerable spatial variation so that the final result will be interesting: 6/28/1980. We know the temperature at 1030 locations, as shown below:

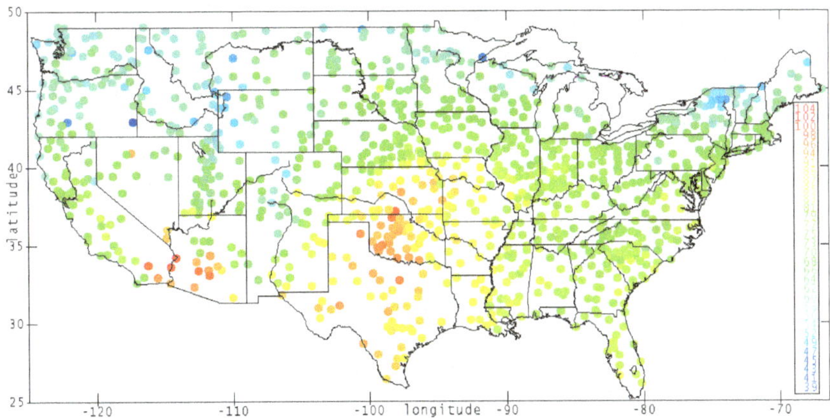

Figure 18. NDP-070 Temperatures on 6/28/1980

We could simply make the spots bigger...

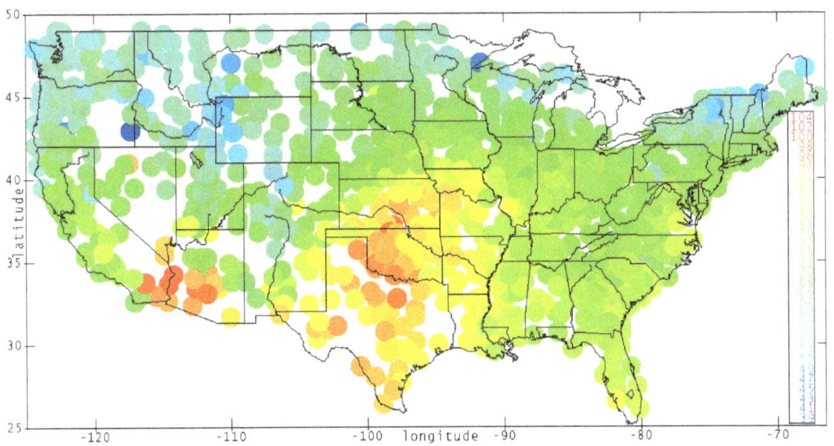

Figure 19. Bigger Spots

...but this hardly seems adequate.

<u>2D Interpolation</u>

There are many algorithms for two-dimensional interpolation of data. We will consider three of these: inverse distance, kriging, and relaxation. The first and third algorithm can be accomplished with TP2, which was used to produce these spot plots (see Appendix A). The first and second can be accomplished with Tecplot™, which is an excellent tool (https://tecplot.com/).

The results of inverse distance interpolation are shown in this next figure:

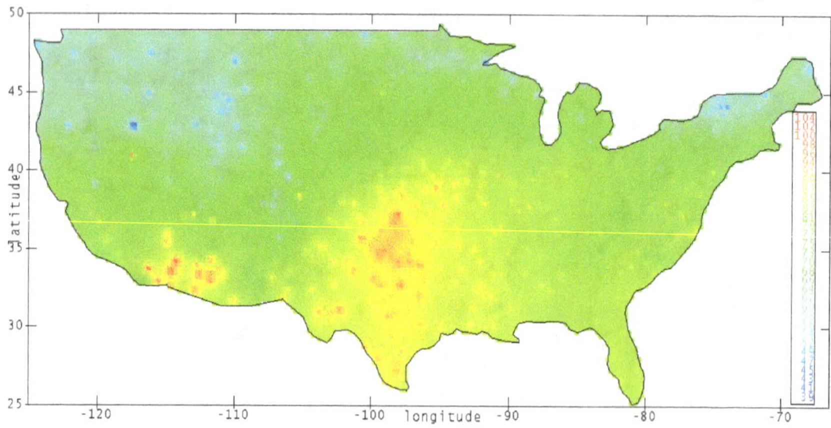

Figure 20. Inverse Distance Interpolation

This isn't too bad but it isn't too good either. Perhaps a little smoothing (averaging surrounding points) would help, as we see in this next figure.

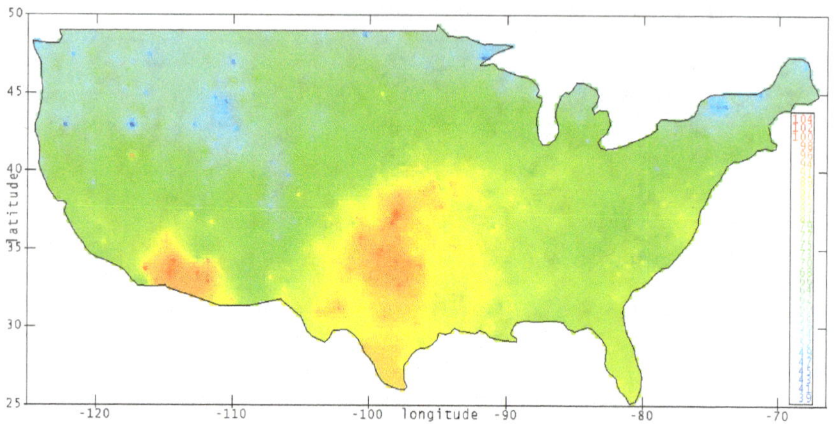

Figure 21. Smoothed Results

The effect is still less than desirable. The localized effects near the border between Wyoming and Idaho plus near the border of California and Arizona have been washed out, as has the blue spot in northern Wisconsin. We visually assume the data from these fairly isolated stations should fill in the surrounding area but is that perception really scientific? This is not an insignificant question when it comes to analyzing climate data. Does "looks right" really imply "is right"? If we are using purely mathematical algorithms not based on any particular physics, then the answer is, "perhaps not".

This next figure shows what we get with kriging. [Note: There are countless articles on the Web devoted to inverse distance and kriging, which describe the formulas and calculations. See Appendix C for more on kriging.]

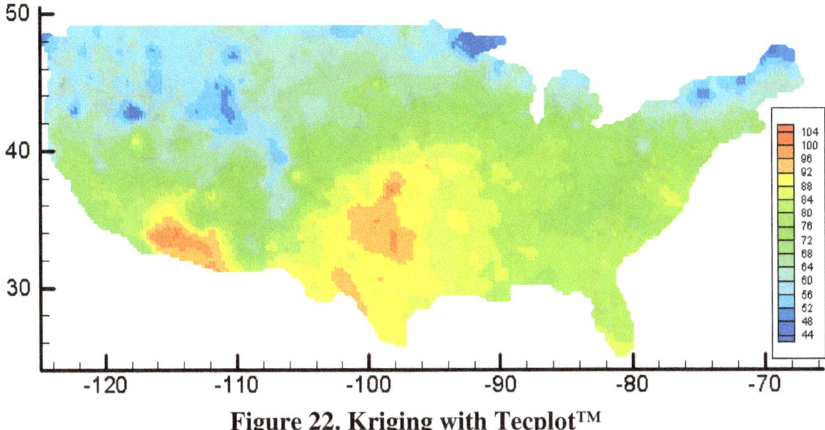

Figure 22. Kriging with Tecplot™

This is a much better result and so you can immediately see why there is so much discussion on the Web about the merits of this and other more elaborate algorithms. We could break the domain down into triangles, as shown in this next figure:

Figure 23. Triangulated Domain

With the domain in this form, we could linearly interpolate over each triangle. Tecplot™ will create the triangles from the points (see menu > data > triangulate) and then interpolate over the domain by flood-filled contours within each triangular element. To accomplish this, check [x] contours; then menu > fields > contour attributes and select flood for the triangular zone. To outline each triangle in black check [x] mesh, then menu > fields > mesh attributes and set the mesh color to black. The layout and data files can be found in the online

15

archive accompanying this text in the examples\triangulation folder. The online archive can be found at the link beneath the Preface. The result is shown here:

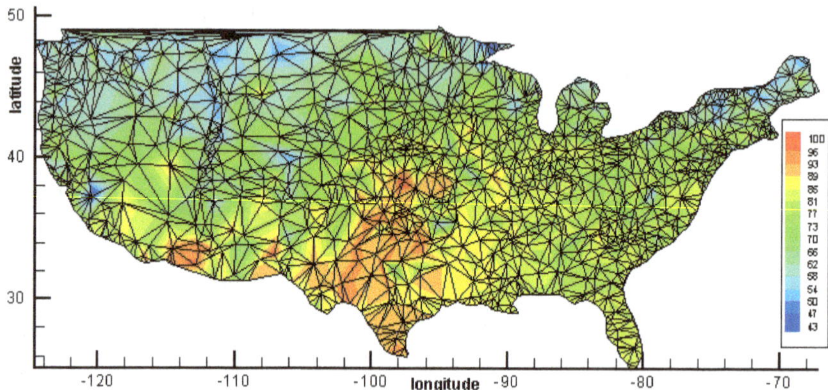

Figure 24. Linear Interpolation within Triangular Elements

<u>Average Temperature</u>

One big question related to climate data is: how to determine the average? One way would be to assign weights to each station. We could add one-third the area of each triangle to each of the three nodes and add these over the domain. The results are in the spreadsheet and shown below:

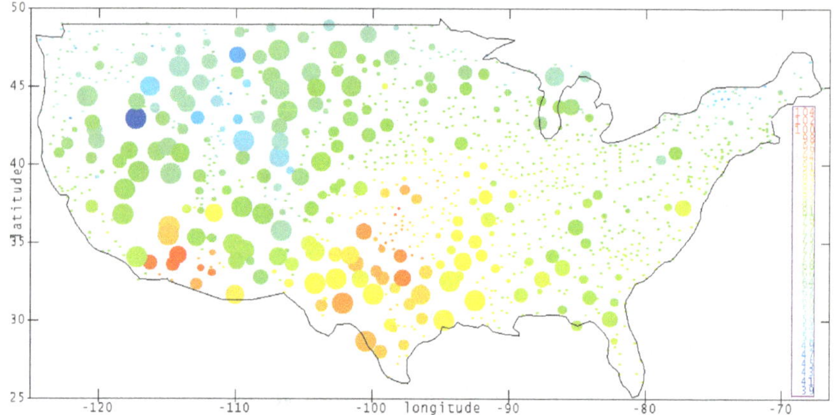

Figure 25. Spot Size Proportional to Area (i.e., Weighted)

At this point you might be wondering where to find such versatile plotting software with so many features? The answer: there was no such thing. That's why I created TPLOT (the first generation of TP2) back in 1980. Every time I needed a new feature or to handle a new file type, I added it. As we are considering weights based on the area associated with each station, rather than simply being concerned with how many stations are reporting data for a given

16

day, we might consider the total area associated with the stations reporting for that day, as some stations are more important than others when calculating an average temperature. Areas for this collection are shown in the figure below:

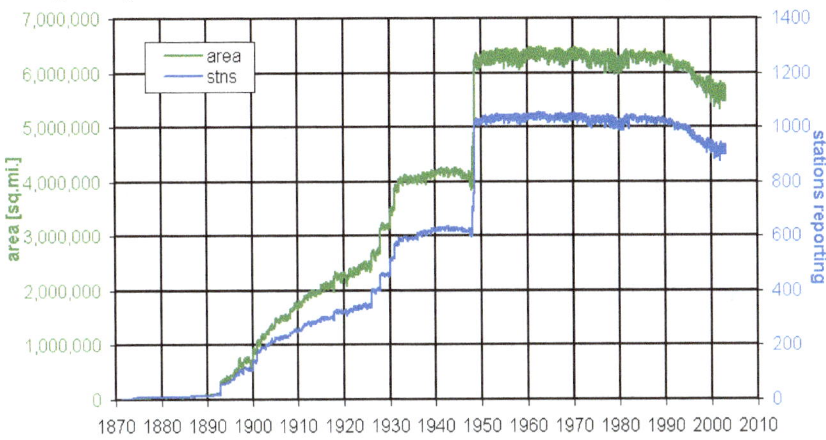

Figure 26. NDP-070 Daily Areas from Stations Reporting

In this case the two (areas and stations reporting) are roughly equivalent. We can use these weights to calculate an average over the "Lower 48". The results are shown in this next figure:

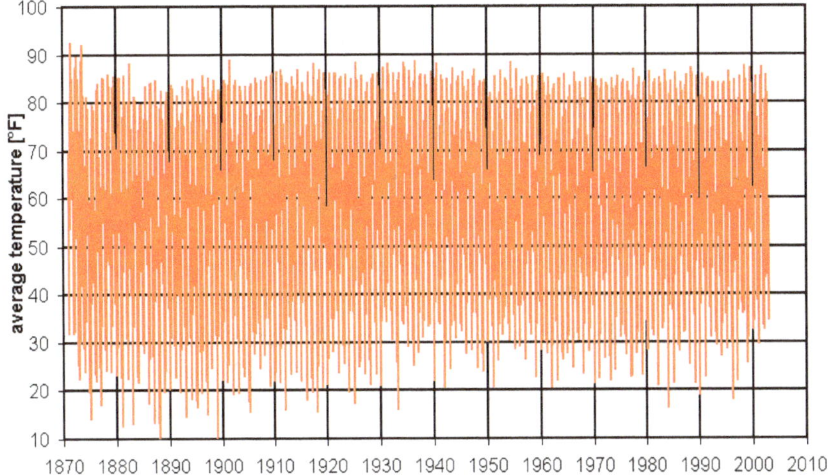

Figure 27. NDP-070 Daily Average Temperature (Area Weighted)

We can't tell much from this last figure except that the temperature does vary considerably, even when considering the area-weighted average.

We can get a little better understanding of this data by separating the data into months:

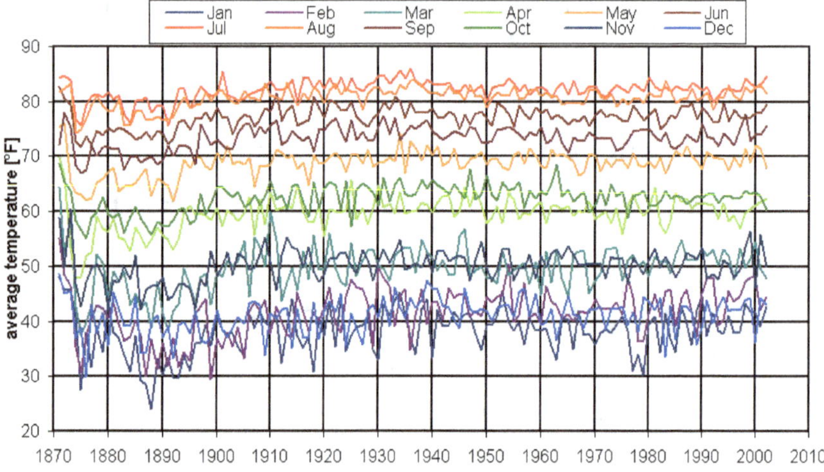

Figure 28. NDP-070 Average Temperature by Month

The anomalies (greater variability) before 1900 are likely due to fewer stations reporting and not climatic. This is more apparent when plotting the yearly average:

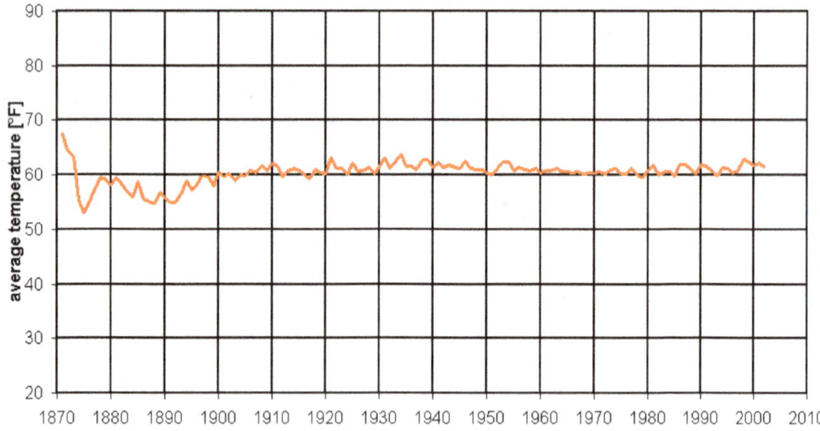

Figure 29. NDP-070 Yearly Average Temperature

We now move on to the big data set.

Chapter 3. GSOD Collection

By far the most extensive and useful collection of bulk meteorological data is the Global [Surface] Summary Of [the] Day (GSOD), gathered by the Federal Climate Complex (FCC) in cooperation with the World Meteorological Organization (WMO) World Weather Watch Program (WWWP). The GSOD is archived at the National Climate Data Center (NCDC), which is operated by the National Oceanographic and Atmospheric Administration (NOAA), at the web address below:

https://www.ncdc.noaa.gov/

NOAA is in the process of shifting this repository to the National Centers for Environmental Information (NCEI), which may redirect you to this web address:

https://www.ncei.noaa.gov/

The bulk data (i.e., the real gold mine) is currently located at the following web address:

ftp://ftp.ncdc.noaa.gov/pub/data/gsod

You will need ftp access to obtain this data, which consists of 107+ UNIX tarballs. How you manage that depends on your machine and operating system. Be aware that this varies with the version of Windows™ you are using too. In some cases you can access ftp using Windows Explorer (the file management tool, not the web browser). On other versions, you might be able to access ftp data with Internet Explorer (the now-discontinued web browser before Edge™). You may need to explore several options. Also beware that not all Internet providers allow ftp access. We recently switched from Xfinity™ to T-Moble™, only to discover that you can't get ftp access over the latter; so we had to switch back. That's the first time I have encountered such a problem. If you exhaust all recommended solutions for your operating system, check with your carrier, but don't be surprised if the guy at the shop who just sells the latest iPhone has no idea what ftp is or why anyone would want to do anything besides mindlessly watch TikTok videos until your brain melts.

When you finally get access to the ftp site it will look like this:

There is a folder for each year. This is the 2023 folder. At the bottom you will find gsod_2023.tar. All of the other files are for individual stations; for example, 01001-99999 is the first in this list. This and the other station files are gzipped, as indicated by the file extension .gz. If you get the .tar file for the year it will contain all of the .op.gz files. You must copy every .tar file in order to build your own repository. I don't know of any shortcuts or *.tar copy options, but such may be possible. This is presumably a UNIX machine and there may be a shortcut using that operating system.

You will also need the file that contains the location of the stations, which is in another folder, as indicated on the website. This file is named: isd-history.csv.

The contents of gsod_2023.tar as viewed with WinZip™ are shown below:

Name	Type	Modified	Size	Ratio	Packed
010010-99999-2023.op.gz	WinZip File	10/23/2023 12:57 PM	8,790	0%	8,790
010014-99999-2023.op.gz	WinZip File	10/23/2023 12:57 PM	4,923	0%	4,923
010020-99999-2023.op.gz	WinZip File	10/23/2023 12:57 PM	282	0%	282
010030-99999-2023.op.gz	WinZip File	10/23/2023 12:57 PM	852	0%	852
010060-99999-2023.op.gz	WinZip File	10/23/2023 12:57 PM	372	0%	372
010070-99999-2023.op.gz	WinZip File	10/23/2023 12:57 PM	6,731	0%	6,731
010080-99999-2023.op.gz	WinZip File	10/23/2023 12:57 PM	6,470	0%	6,470
010090-99999-2023.op.gz	WinZip File	10/23/2023 12:57 PM	490	0%	490
010100-99999-2023.op.gz	WinZip File	10/23/2023 12:57 PM	6,049	0%	6,049
010110-99999-2023.op.gz	WinZip File	10/23/2023 12:57 PM	434	0%	434
010150-99999-2023.op.gz	WinZip File	10/23/2023 12:57 PM	566	0%	566
010160-99999-2023.op.gz	WinZip File	10/23/2023 12:57 PM	327	0%	327
010170-99999-2023.op.gz	WinZip File	10/23/2023 12:57 PM	305	0%	305
010200-99999-2023.op.gz	WinZip File	10/23/2023 12:57 PM	378	0%	378
010230-99999-2023.op.gz	WinZip File	10/23/2023 12:57 PM	5,725	0%	5,725
010231-99999-2023.op.gz	WinZip File	10/23/2023 12:57 PM	5,349	0%	5,349
010240-99999-2023.op.gz	WinZip File	10/23/2023 12:57 PM	240	0%	240
010250-99999-2023.op.gz	WinZip File	10/23/2023 12:57 PM	6,147	0%	6,147
010260-99999-2023.op.gz	WinZip File	10/23/2023 12:57 PM	9,179	0%	9,179
010270-99999-2023.op.gz	WinZip File	10/23/2023 12:58 PM	3,955	0%	3,955
010280-99999-2023.op.gz	WinZip File	10/23/2023 12:58 PM	1,614	0%	1,614
010300-99999-2023.op.gz	WinZip File	10/23/2023 12:58 PM	442	0%	442
010330-99999-2023.op.gz	WinZip File	10/23/2023 12:58 PM	423	0%	423
010350-99999-2023.op.gz	WinZip File	10/23/2023 12:58 PM	398	0%	398
010370-99999-2023.op.gz	WinZip File	10/23/2023 12:58 PM	441	0%	441

Selected 0 files, 0 bytes — Total 12251 files, 75,026KB

As shown at the bottom, the 2023 tarball contains 12,251 station files totaling 75,026KB. The collection of 1929 through 2023 is approximately 877,000 files. Compressed these files occupy about 5GB. "Please email them to me" is not an option so don't ask.

While it may be possible to untar and ungzip all of these into a folder on your machine, it isn't very practical. I have extracted a single year to analyze it and have extracted a single station from every year, but never all of the files at once. I find it more practical to untar and ungzip each station for each year, read, and delete it on the fly by building that capability into my software for analyzing the data. This is rather complicated but you can find the source code for untar.c and gzip.c free on the Web.

This first figure shows the location of the GSOD stations:

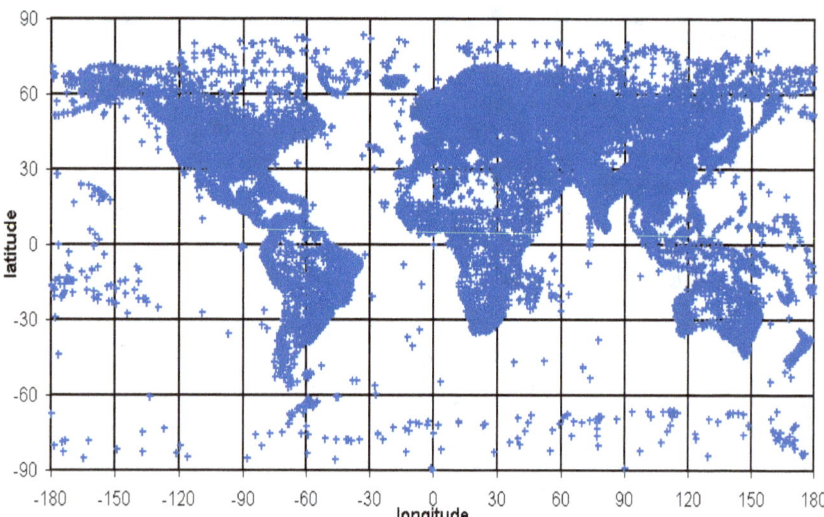

Figure 30. GSOD Station Locations

Not surprisingly, the number of stations reporting data varies significantly over time, as shown in this next figure:

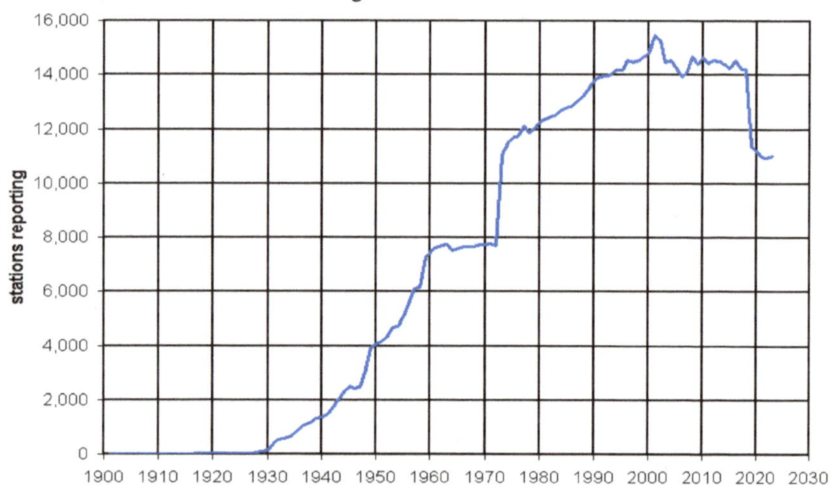

Figure 31. GSOD Number of Stations Reporting

While there is considerable data in this collection before 1973, the more complete coverage doesn't begin until after that year. For this reason, I limit most of my global analyses to this time period (1973-present).

Another way of looking at the data coverage by station is shown in this next figure in which the size of the spots for each station are proportional to the quantity of available data for that station.

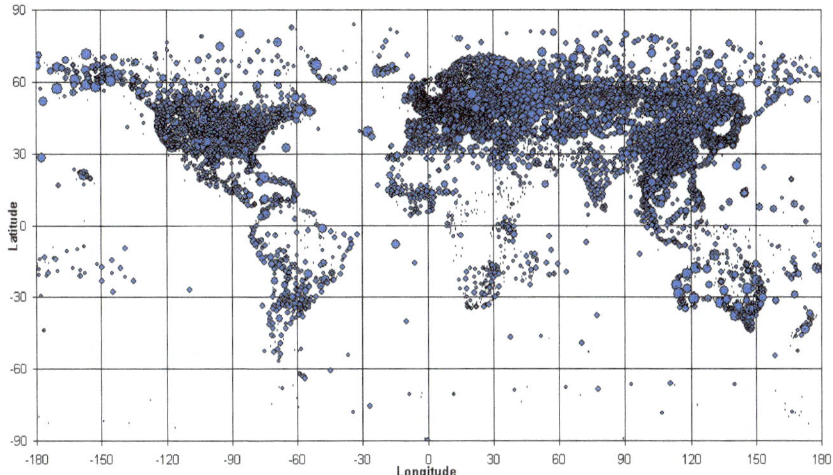

Figure 32. GSOD Quantity of Available Data Per Station

Consider a recent hot day, which generated a lot of press:

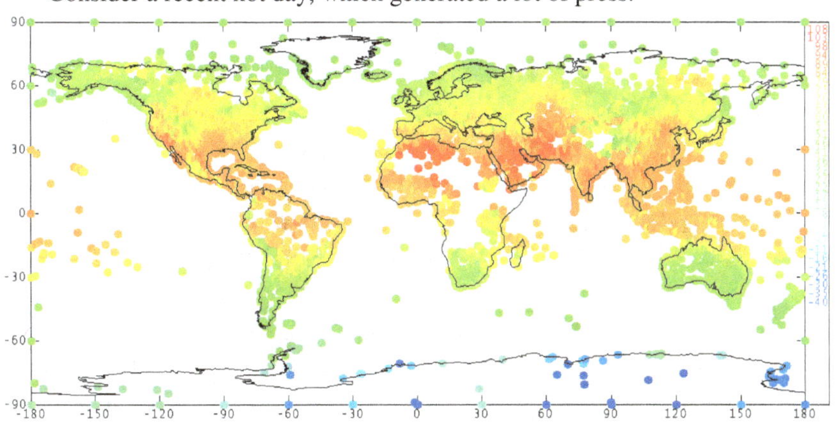

Figure 33. GSOD Station Temperatures for 7/1/2023

There is adequate coverage calculate a reasonable average for the land areas but not the sea. There are satellite temperature estimates for the oceans, but as we will discuss later, the temperature of the water and the air just above the water may be significantly different. As we are considering temperatures of the air over the land and not temperatures of the land itself (i.e., dirt), we should not combine these with temperatures of the water. Satellites do not *measure* the temperature of the seas; rather, they *calculate* it, which involves assumptions.

23

We could triangulate the world, incorporating the stations, as before:

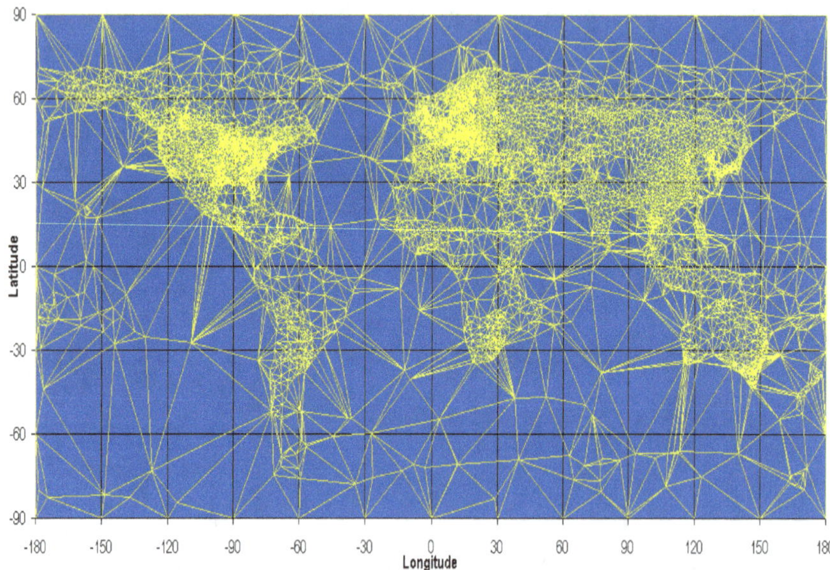

Figure 34. Global Triangulation Based on GSOD Stations

We can linearly interpolate over the triangles to arrive at a temperature map:

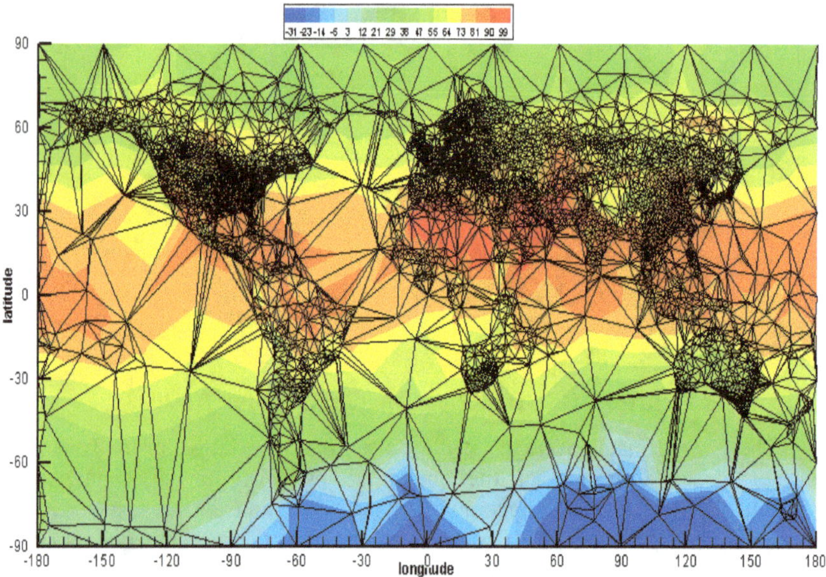

Figure 35. Global Temps by Linear Interp. within Triangles 7/1/2023

24

Again, we can calculate areas and assign one-third to each node, accumulating these over the domain to arrive at area weights for each station.

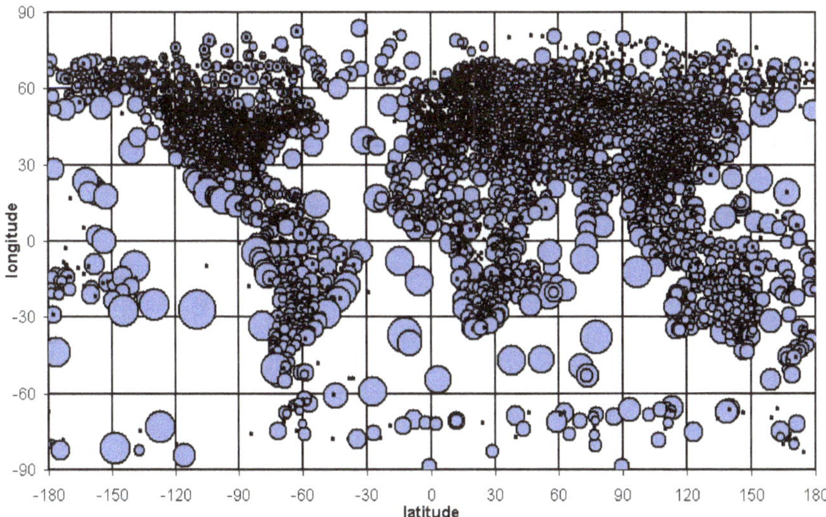

Figure 36. GSOD Station Area Weights

Using these weights (from the triangular mesh), we can calculate a global average temperature, which will be more accurate than a simple arithmetic average that doesn't account for the very uneven spatial distribution of the meteorological stations.

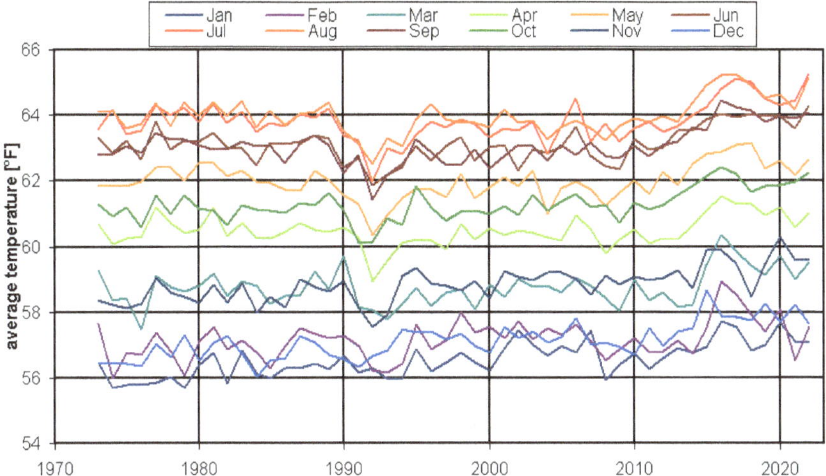

Figure 37. GSOD Global Average Monthly Temperatures Using Mesh

We can also plot the yearly average temperature calculated in this same way and on the same scale as the monthly:

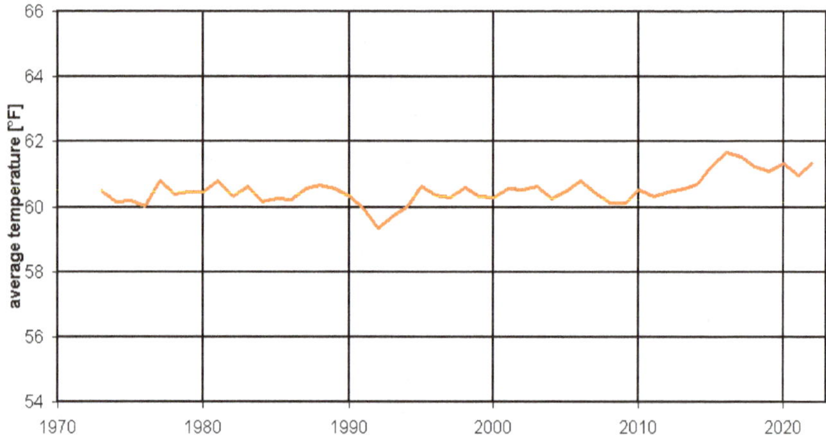

Figure 38. GSOD Global Average Yearly Temperatures Using Mesh

Instead of area weights based on the triangular mesh, we can use the inverse distance method (see Appendix B) to calculate global temperatures.

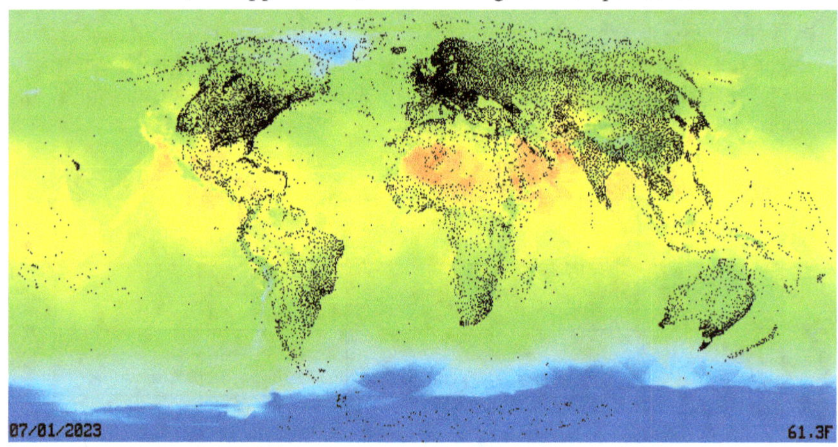

Figure 39. Global Temperatures by Inverse Distance 7/1/2023

When averaging these temperatures calculated over the surface of the Earth, it is essential to consider the actual corresponding areas on the surface of a sphere and not on a flatten projection of the globe. The band of temperatures along the top and bottom of the figure above (i.e., near the poles) represent a tiny area compared to the same width band in the middle (i.e., near the equator). No flat projection (e.g., Mercator) accurately represents a sphere. See Appendix D for map projections.

This is the same result as the previous figure only using the Mollweide projection (my personal favorite):

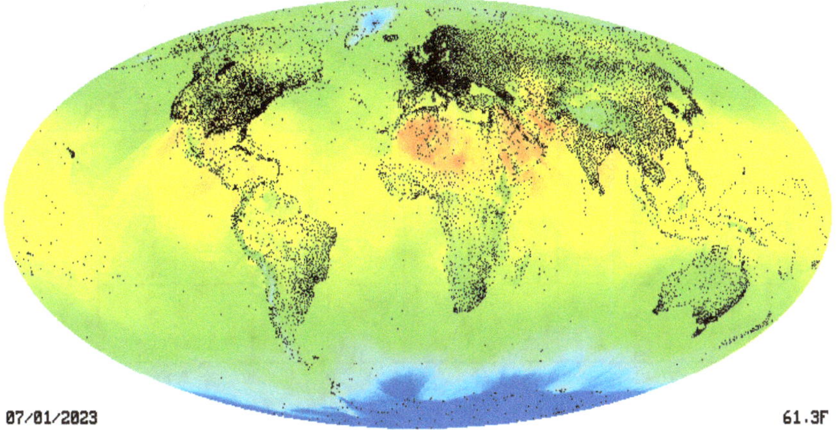

Figure 40. Global Temperatures by Inverse Distance 7/1/2023

Using this algorithm (inverse distance, see Appendix B for details), and the GSOD data set, we obtain the following monthly average temperatures:

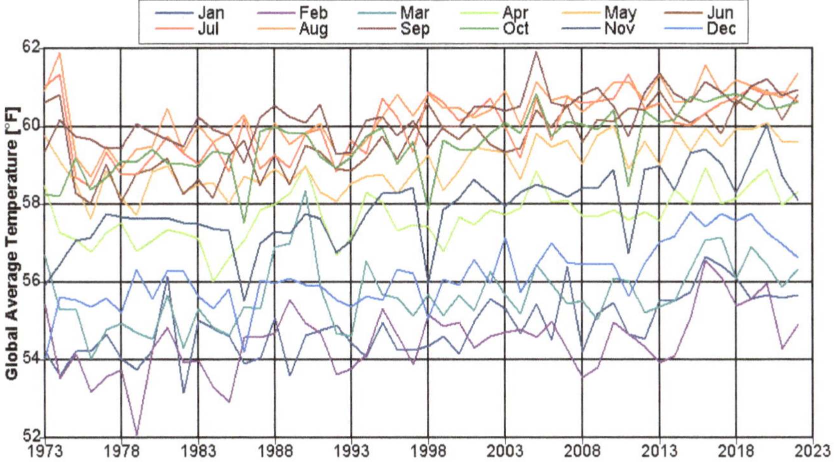

Figure 41. Global Avg. Monthly Temps (GSDOD + inverse distance)

Note the differences between the averages calculated using the inverse distance method and the triangular mesh. We will discuss this more in the next chapter. In this case it seems that the inverse distance method is more sensitive (i.e., uncertain outcome) to missing or sparse data compared to the mesh method. The meshes were optimized based on the stations reporting data.

This next figure shows the yearly average temperatures:

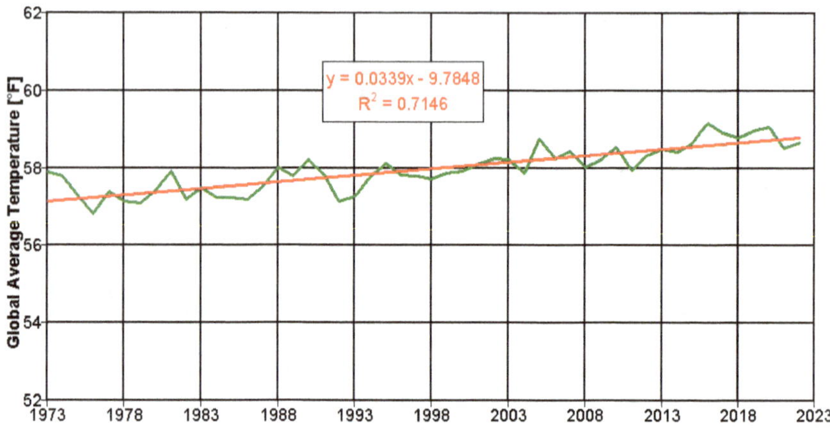

Figure 42. Yearly Values - Same Data - Same Method - Same Scale

We use the same scale (vertical axis) to present the yearly averages so as to avoid any misleading exaggeration. The linear trend is +0.0339 °F/year or +0.0188 °C/year or a *warming* of 1.88 °C/century. This result is consistent with many publications on global warming. As we shall see in the next chapter, the inverse distance method tends to stretch out the influence of individual stations in a nonlinear way (e.g., a falling exponential). Kriging also does this same type of stretching and, in fact, uses e^{-r} in the calculations. This is stretching (i.e., exponential decay) is not consistent with the physics which governs the distribution of heat energy (and thus temperature) throughout the atmosphere. When we use a technique consistent with the physics, we get a slope of 1.38 °C/century or about 36% less, which is closer to some other publications.

Chapter 4. Spatial Gaps

We next consider the spatial distribution of meteorological data. While 28,000 stations may sound like a lot, they are rather clumped—at least from a global point of view when we're hoping to accurately calculate the average temperature over the whole surface of the Earth. We are conceptually limited and also constrained by the flat pages of a book so that map projections are essential to our understanding. This first figure shows the GSOD stations sprinkled over a Mollweide projection of the Earth:

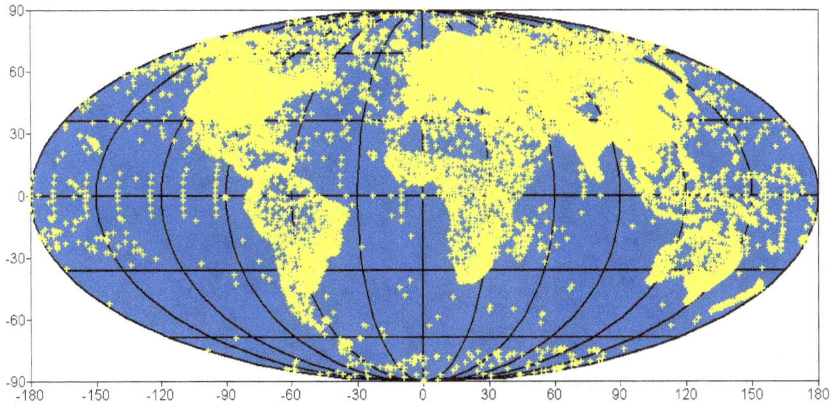

Figure 43. GSOD Stations on Mollweide

The land is covered quite well, except in North Africa where we don't expect a lot of variation anyway. The glaring lack of information is over the World's oceans. As previously discussed, remote sensing (i.e., via satellite) is not likely to provide accurate measurements for the air temperature over the seas and to combine any other (e.g., water surface effective radiative temperature) with the air temperatures over the land would be inconsistent, inappropriate, and likely misleading.

We could just consider the land and ignore the ocean, as in this figure:

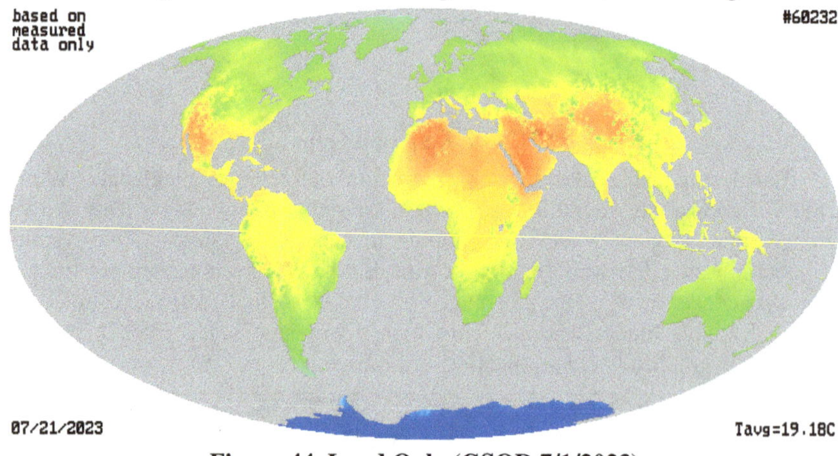

Figure 44. Land Only (GSOD 7/1/2023)

or just the oceans and ignore the land:

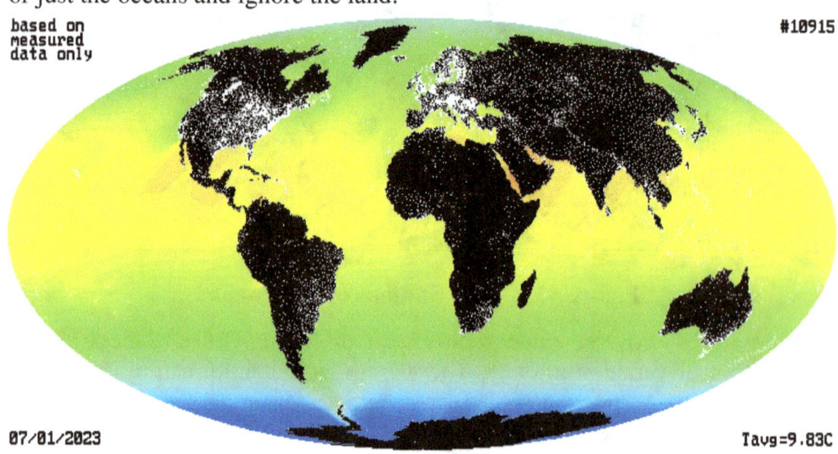

Figure 45. Sea Only (GSOD 7/1/2023)

The problem is that 71% of the Earth's surface is covered with water and it makes a big difference whether you consider this area or not. There is no obvious, clear-cut, unassailable answer to this question. Strategically, this issue (i.e., land/sea) is not that different from the spatial disparity over land and sparsity of data before 1973. We simply don't have exhaustive (i.e., complete and perfect) data. We must then do the best we can with what we've got and humbly present the results as tentative. Sadly, this is not often the case. Climate "results" are most often delivered with the utmost arrogance.

Perhaps the best thing we can do is to fill the spatial gaps *naturally*. The question then becomes: what is natural? What drives the atmospheric temperatures (and energy within the air) near the surface of the Earth? Certainly, heat input from the Sun and heat loss to space. If we were to *calculate* (i.e., *model*) this exchange of energy explicitly, then we would no longer be considering *real* (i.e., *measured*) data. We would be another step farther away from the facts into the vast wasteland of speculation. While it is rarely discussed in the mainstream media, you can get whatever answer you want by "tuning" a model to achieve a desired outcome. This is why I place no stock in climate "models". When great effort (and expense) are invested in developing a "model" there is considerable pressure to "tune" it so as to please those doling out the money. I am personally quite suspicious of anything said by someone whose continued employment and income depends on telling an approved narrative.

What else impacts air temperatures over the face of the Earth? Certainly wind has a big effect. We will discuss wind data in a subsequent chapter but suffice it to say at this point that there are fewer stations consistently reporting wind speed and direction than there are reporting temperature so that the same quandary exists regarding spatial sparsity for wind data. Rain (precipitation) and evaporation also impact surface air temperatures. Precipitation data is perhaps more questionable (based on considerable specific measured experience with the TVA reservoir system) than wind data.

While we might incorporate other meteorological data in our calculation of temperatures, it is safe to say that this would tend to increase the uncertainty rather than decreasing it. Therefore, we endeavor to do the best we can with the temperature data alone—at least for the purpose of distributing that temperature over the surface of the Earth where there are no meteorological stations reporting. What have we seen thus far? At least visually, it appears that linear interpolation over the triangular grid looks more reasonable than either point method (i.e., inverse distance or kriging).

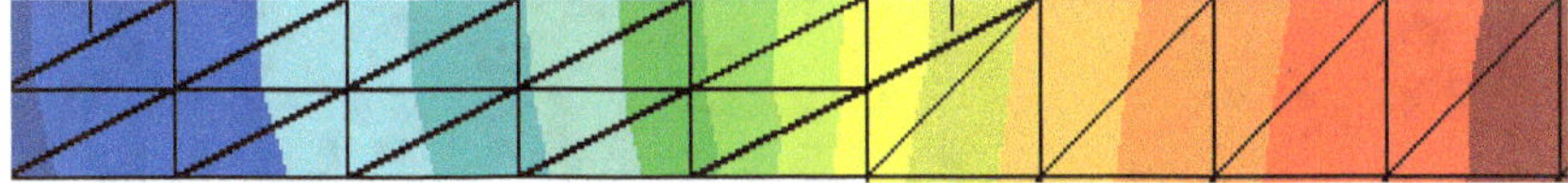

Figure 46. Conduction within Triangular Elements

What does a two-dimensional linear distribution of temperature such as illustrated first with the triangular mesh for the "Lower 48" and then the whole Earth plus in the figure above imply? In short: conduction. The following is Laplace's equation in three-dimensional Cartesian coordinates:

$$\frac{\partial^2 T}{\partial x^2} + \frac{\partial^2 T}{\partial y^2} + \frac{\partial^2 T}{\partial z^2} = 0 \tag{4.1}$$

This partial differential equation governs heat conduction. It also governs diffusion and inviscid flow (i.e., very low viscosity or high Reynolds number). If any partial differential equation might represent the spreading of temperature across the surface of the Earth, this would be it. While it isn't *exact* in this case and it doesn't account for *every* process, at least it doesn't explicitly (or implicitly) bring in extraneous factors or rely on sweeping assumptions, which we should avoid. The problem with sweeping assumptions is that we might be tempted to accept one that reinforces a particular narrative while rejecting another contrary to the favored storyline.

As it turns out, had we taken the "Lower 48" mesh or the Earth mesh and fed this into a two-dimensional steady-state heat conduction (or mass diffusion) model with the station reported temperatures set as constant boundary conditions, we would get the exact same color map that Tecplot™ drew for us by contour-filling the triangles. Could there be a more natural way of filling in the spatial gaps having fewer potentially spurious assumptions? No.

Figure 47. Tessellated Sphere

Any attempt to numerically solve Laplace's equation begins with a grid. The obvious choice for the Globe is a tessellated sphere (shown in the preceding figure). This next figure is a closer look:

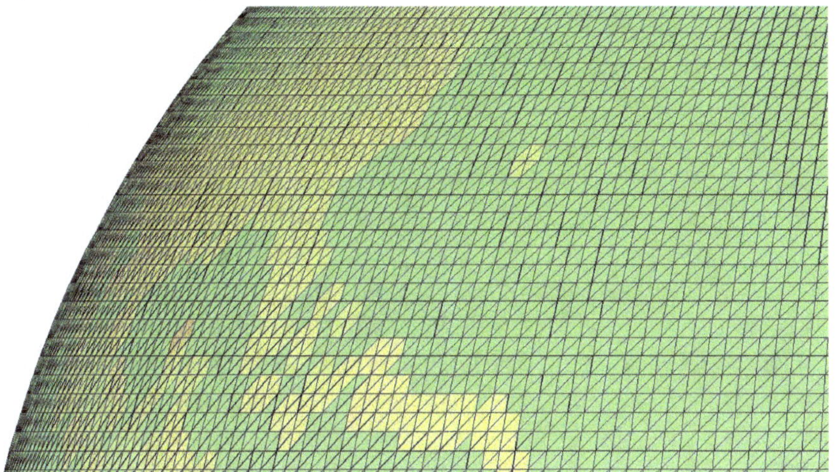

Figure 48. Tessellated Sphere (closer)

This particular tessellation consists of 64,082 nodes and 128,880 triangular elements. The setup is simple: each station is attached to the nearest node. If a node is linked to more than one station, these are averaged. This only occurs for a very small subset of the total. Nodes attached to a station are "fixed points" while those not attached to a station are "free". After fixing these conditions and initializing the rest to some reasonable value, we simply solve the domain as with any other implementation of Laplace's equation. Gauss-Seidel or Successive Over-Relaxation (SOR) works equally well and either is simple to implement. The global average is easy to calculate, as the nodes are all equally spaced. (see Appendix F for more details on tessellation)

Spatial Distortion

There is no spatial distortion with this approach because we are using a sphere for the calculations. We simply read the GSOD tar files and step through time, solving this same problem over-and-over again. We can even write out the 3D finite element solution, perhaps on the first of each month. We may want to create an animation of the temperatures and so some map projection is necessary. We can map the global values onto the projection without distorting the result (i.e., local or average temperatures). I prefer the Mollweide projection and have archived a 720x360 pixel temperature map for every day from 1/1/1973 to the present in yearly GIFs plus a collective GIF with the first of each month.

The resulting map for this same day of interest is shown below:

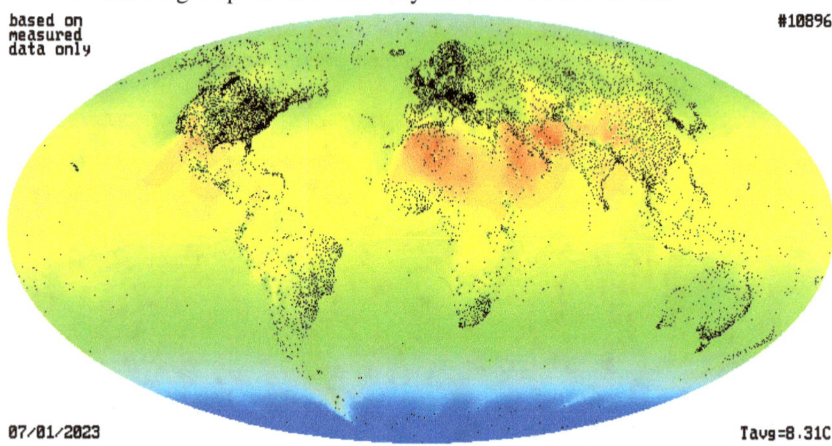

Figure 49. Global Temps Solving Laplace's Equation Using GSOD Data

The same information with the other palette is shown here:

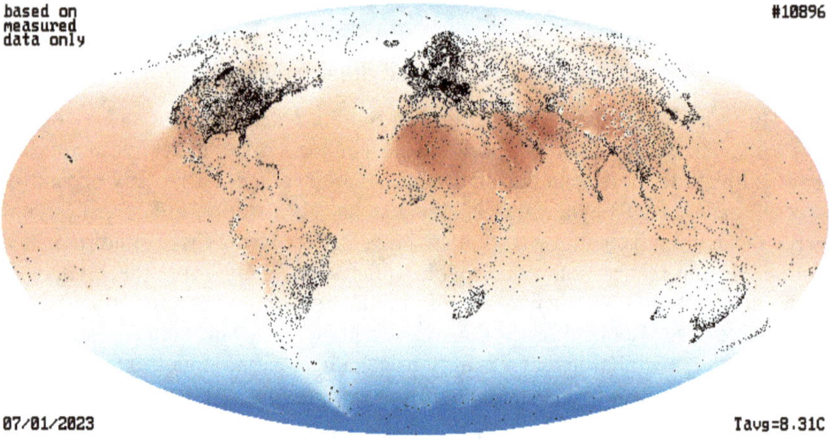

Figure 50. Same Information with Different Palette

It is a simple matter to run through all of the GSOD data from 1973 to the present using this approach and come up with an estimate for the average global temperature—all without using any particular "model" and the countless implicit presumptions that would come with such a model, most notably "tuning" to achieve some desired end result.

Chapter 5. Global Trends

This next figure shows the global average temperature per month over the period of record for which the GSOD contains most of the meteorological stations reporting data (i.e., 1973-present).

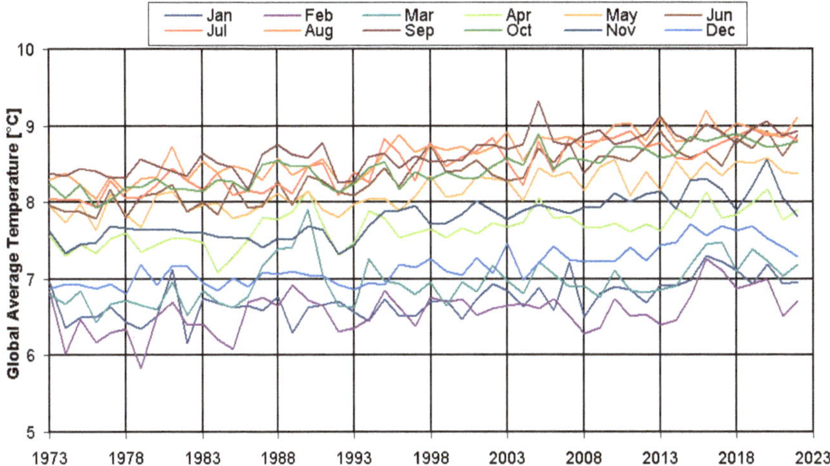

Figure 51. Global Temps Solving Laplace's Eqn. Using GSOD Data

The same data, only yearly averages, is shown in this next figure:

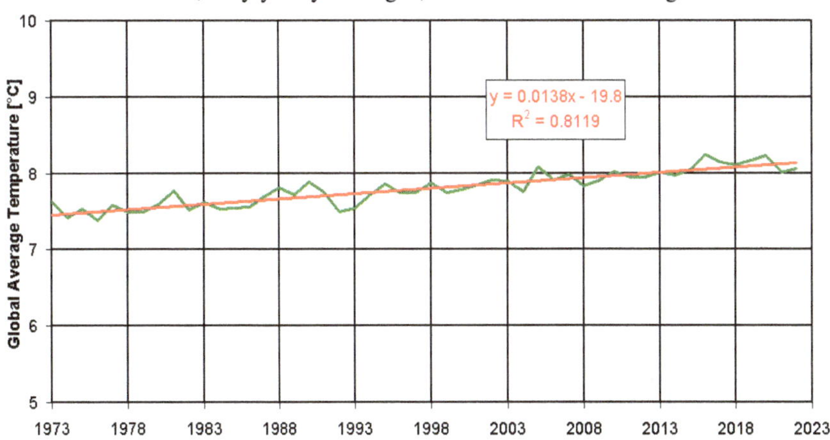

Figure 52. Same Results on Yearly Basis with Trend (Same Scale)

At last we arrive at the BIG QUESTION: is there any solid empirical evidence (i.e., *actual* measurements) supporting the hypothesis of global warming? Based on this figure, the answer would seem to be: *yes*. The slope of the linear trend line is 0.0138 °C/year or 1.38 °C/century or 1 °C per 72.5 years. The correlation coefficient, R^2 is 81.19%. We have gone to great lengths to arrive at this result without drawing upon algorithms, which might be suspect. Still, assumptions have been made and caveats have been suggested. We offer this result with open hands and mind. The daily values are shown in this next figure.

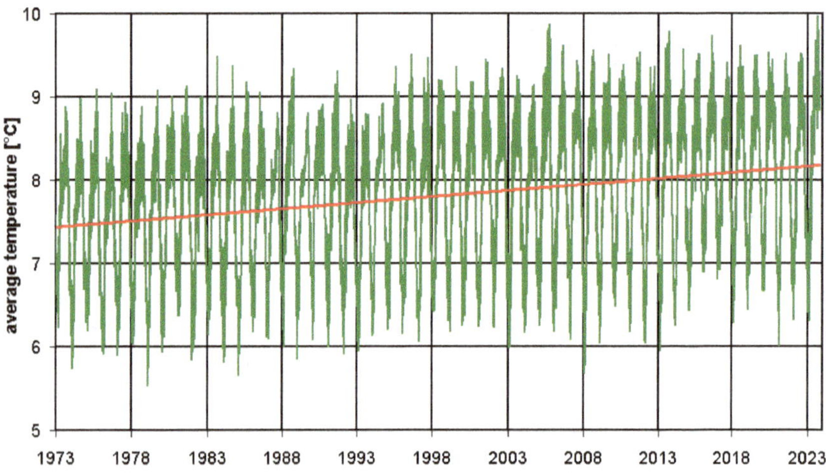

Figure 53. Daily Results (Same Data/Same Algorithm/Same Scale)

The 50-year using this data painted over the Earth with can be seen in Figures 4 and 5 on page iv. This same information flat is shown here:

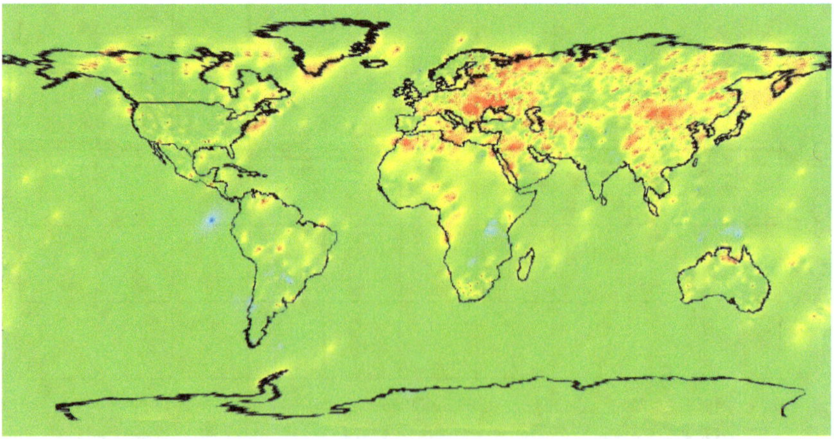

Figure 54. Fifty-Year Global Temperature Trend (Flat)

This same information stretched over a sphere is shown in these next four figures at different rotations:

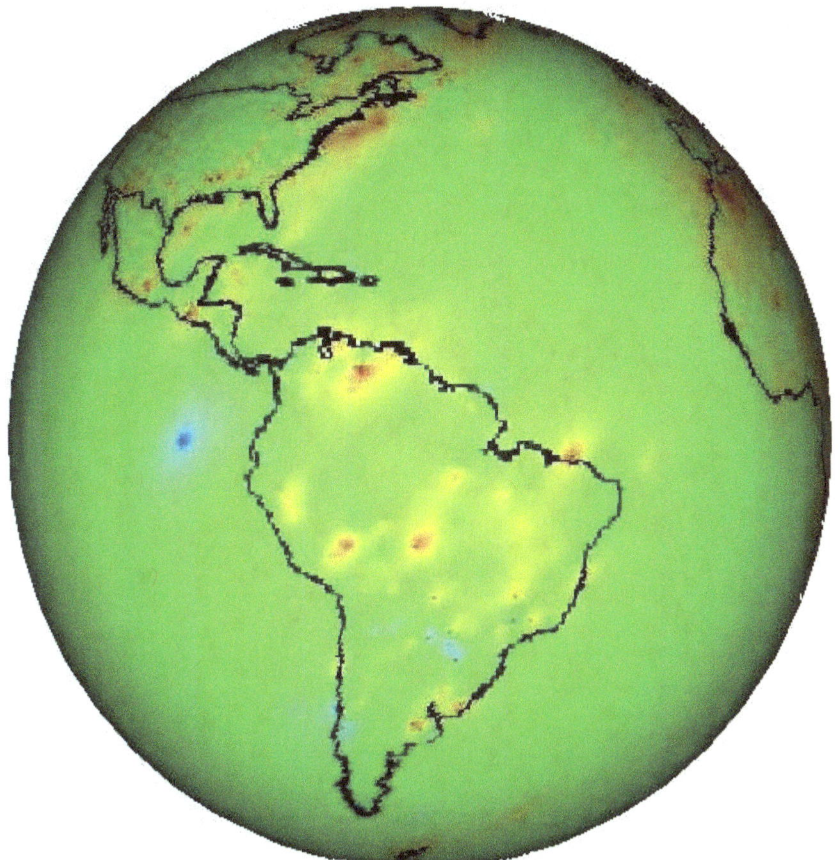

Figure 55. Fifty-Year Temperature Trend

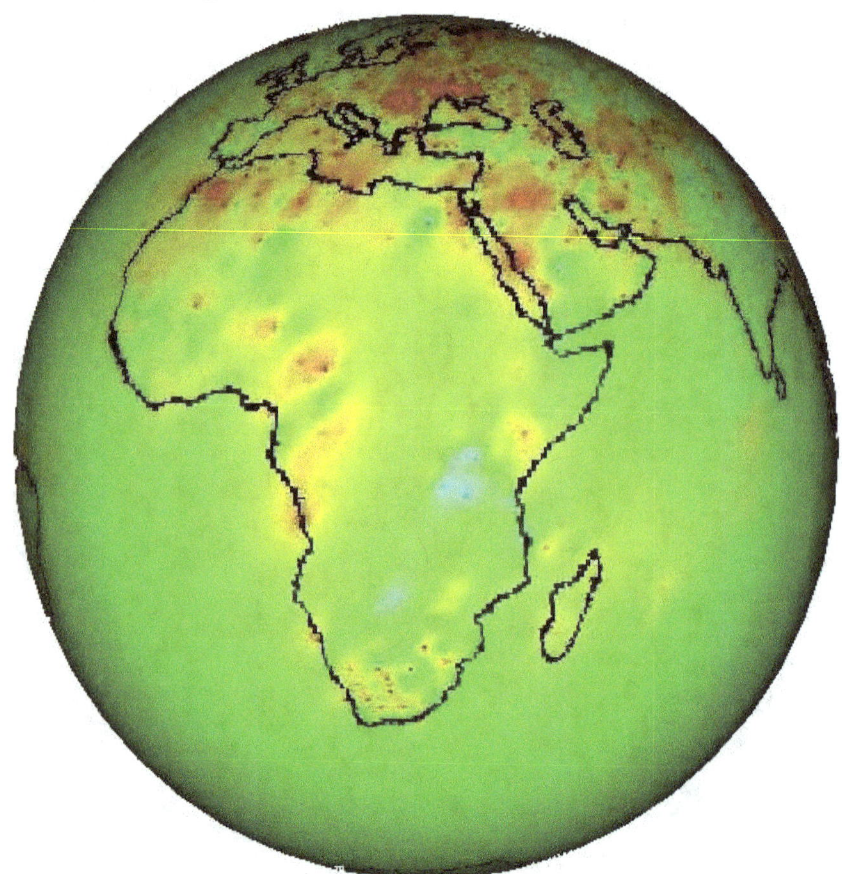

Figure 56. Fifty-Year Temperature Trend

Rotated 180° west...

Figure 57. Fifty-Year Temperature Trend

From the top...

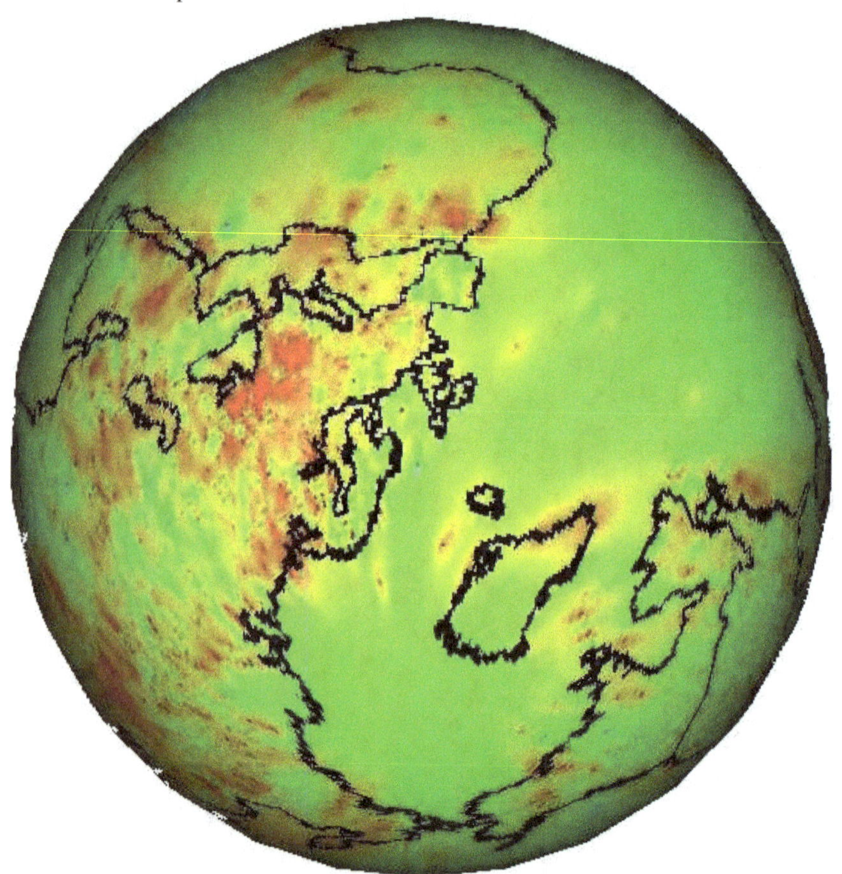

Figure 58. Fifty-Year Temperature Trend331

Chapter 6. Regional Trends

On July 23, 2023 the Goddard Digital Team published a report entitled, "NASA Finds June 2023 Hottest on Record", which contains this figure.[1]

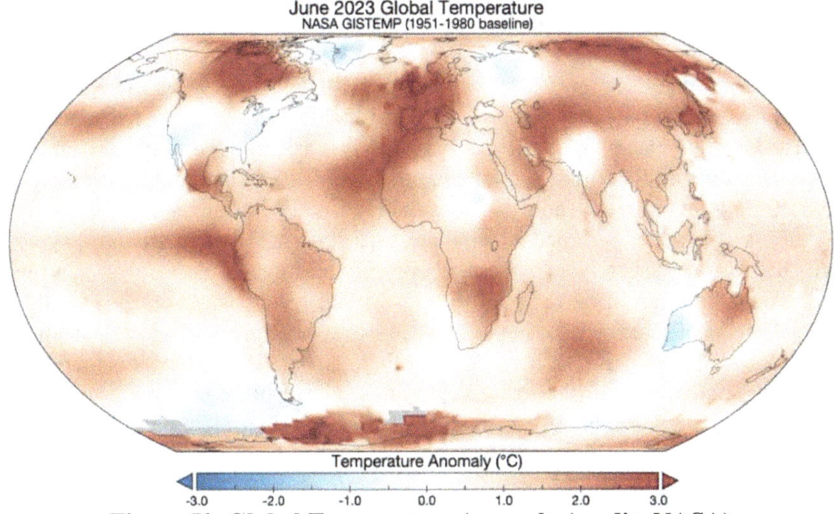

Figure 59. Global Temperature Anomaly (credit: NASA)

In that report, they state:

> This map shows global temperature anomalies for June 2023 according to the GISTEMP analysis by scientists at NASA's Goddard Institute for Space Studies. Most of the world is red due to warm anomalies, with the highest anomalies around Antarctica and Canada. Temperature anomalies reflect how June 2023 compared to the average June temperature from 1951-1980. GISTEMP, NASA's global temperature analysis, is drawn from data collected by weather stations and Antarctic research stations, as well as instruments mounted on ships and ocean buoys. NASA scientists at the Goddard Institute for Space Studies (GISS) in New York analyze these measurements to account for uncertainties in the data and to maintain consistent methods for calculating global average surface temperature differences for every year. These ground-based measurements of surface temperature are consistent with satellite data collected since 2002 by the Atmospheric Infrared Sounder on NASA's Aqua satellite and with other estimates. NASA uses the period from 1951-1980 as a baseline to understand how global temperatures change over time. Independent analyses by the

---

[1] https://www.nasa.gov/centers-and-facilities/goddard/nasa-finds-june-2023-hottest-on-record/

European Union's Copernicus Climate Change Service and NOAA's National Centers for Environmental Information likewise found June 2023 to be the warmest June in their records. *Credits: NASA's Goddard Institute for Space Studies. Editor: Jamie Adkins.*

We see two important details in this statement from NASA:

1) The data come from weather stations, including instruments mounted on ships and buoys, which also describes the GSOD collection.
2) These data are [said to be] consistent with satellite data and other estimates.

Perhaps the most noticeable detail in this figure is that most of the US (i.e., the Lower 48) is blue and so is Western Australia. What does this (blue shading) mean? There's nothing going on in the Lower 48! The glaring dark red spots are in Europe and Asia. There is also a huge red blotch in Northeastern Canada. What does this mean? Well... that's hard to say for sure. One might be tempted to conclude from this official proclamation from NASA that the US has worked hard for a long time to clean up their act as far as CO_2 emissions go; at least, that would be the logical inference from this figure consistent with the anthropogenic global warming narrative. Why are there big red blotches in Canada, Europe, and Asia? One might be tempted to suspect that they *haven't* cleaned up their act. The Asians make no pretence of this but the Europeans and Canadians project an image of innocence. Perhaps there's something going on there that they aren't sharing with the rest of the Planet. Never mind the explanation. Let us set aside any speculation and merely analyze the data more carefully; and to do that, we will go region-by-region.

<u>The Lower 48</u>

We have already looked at this region when we considered the GHCN/NDP-041 Collection in Chapter 1. The GSOD collection contains this and even more data so that we can use it to take a closer look. We have also argued that the tessellation technique and solving Laplace's equation is preferable to the triangular mesh and area-weighted approach.

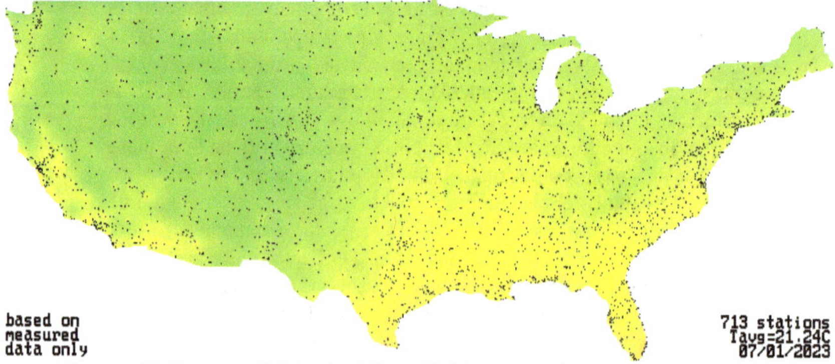

Figure 60. Lower 48/Typical Day/GSOD Data/Tessellation Method

42

The average temperatures for each month are shown in this next figure:

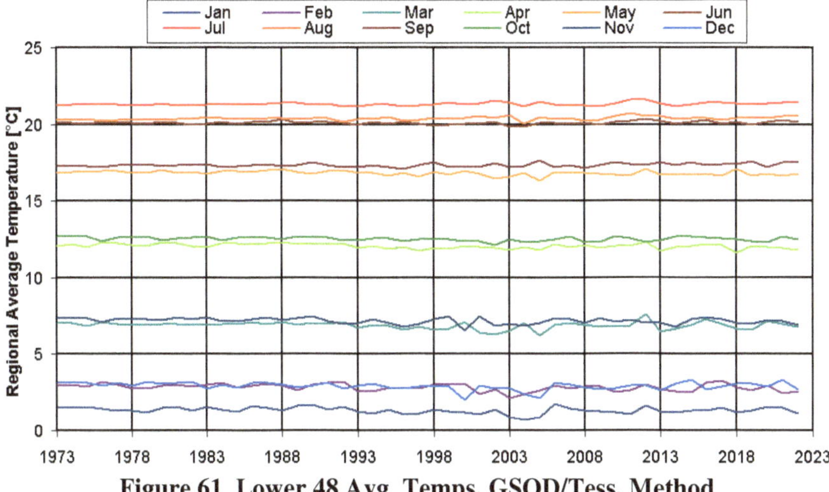

Figure 61. Lower 48 Avg. Temps. GSOD/Tess. Method

The yearly averages are shown in this figure:

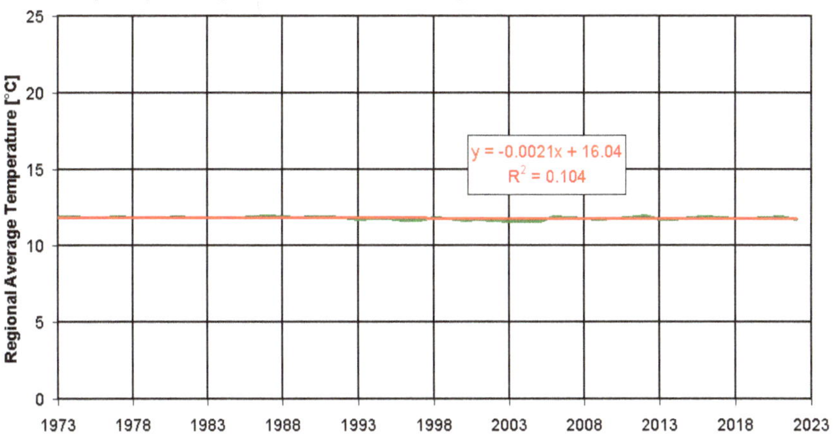

Figure 62. Yearly Values - Same Data - Same Method - Same Scale

The linear trend is –0.0021 °C/year or a ***cooling*** of 0.21 °C/century! This result is consistent with the bluish shading of the region in NASA's figure.

Australia

The Land Down Under was another region shaded mostly in blue on the NASA Naughty List. We can limit our calculations to this island continent as for the Lower 48. There aren't as many stations; however, the terrain is much less diverse too so this isn't a critical limitation of the GSOD collection.

Here we got July 1, 2023 for ya, Mate:

Figure 63. Down Under/GSOD Data/Tessellation Method

Not much happening in this mild "winter" in July below the Equator. The black specks are the reporting station locations. The average temperatures by month are:

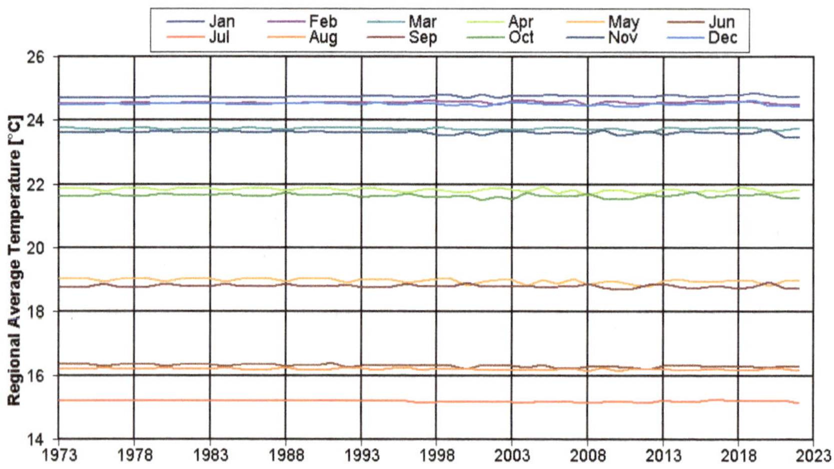

Figure 64. Down Under Avg. Temps. GSOD/Tess. Method

44

The temperatures in Australia are even less variable than in the Lower 48, which isn't surprising considering the terrain. The yearly averages are shown in this next figure:

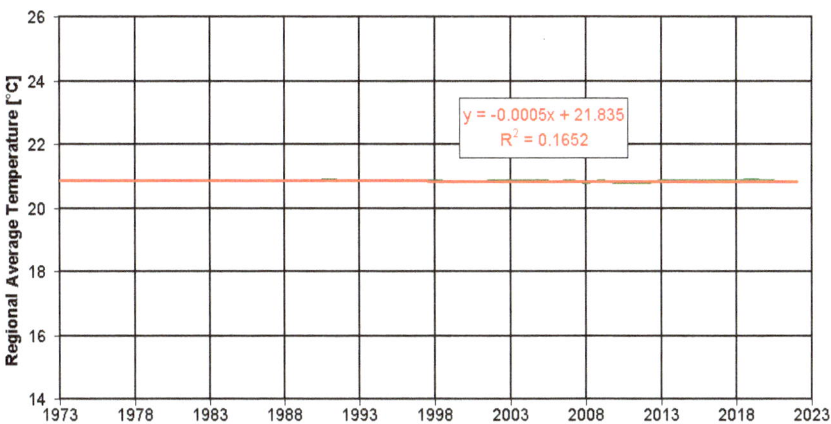

Figure 65. Yearly Values - Same Data - Same Method - Same Scale

The linear trend is –0.0005 °C/year or a ***cooling*** of 0.05 °C/century! This result is consistent with the bluish shading of the region in NASA's figure. Is it any wonder that the Australians are not in a panic over global warming and are resistant to spending mind-boggling sums "addressing the issue"?

<u>South America</u>

South America is another region that shows very little dark red on the NASA "anomaly" map. South America is a vast land consisting of many countries and much diversity. It is literally half of the Western Hemisphere, though you wouldn't know it from watching western media, where it is rarely mentioned. It takes an earthquake killing at least a thousand on an otherwise boring day to get a few minutes on the "World News Tonight".

This same day (7/1/2023) in South America is shown here:

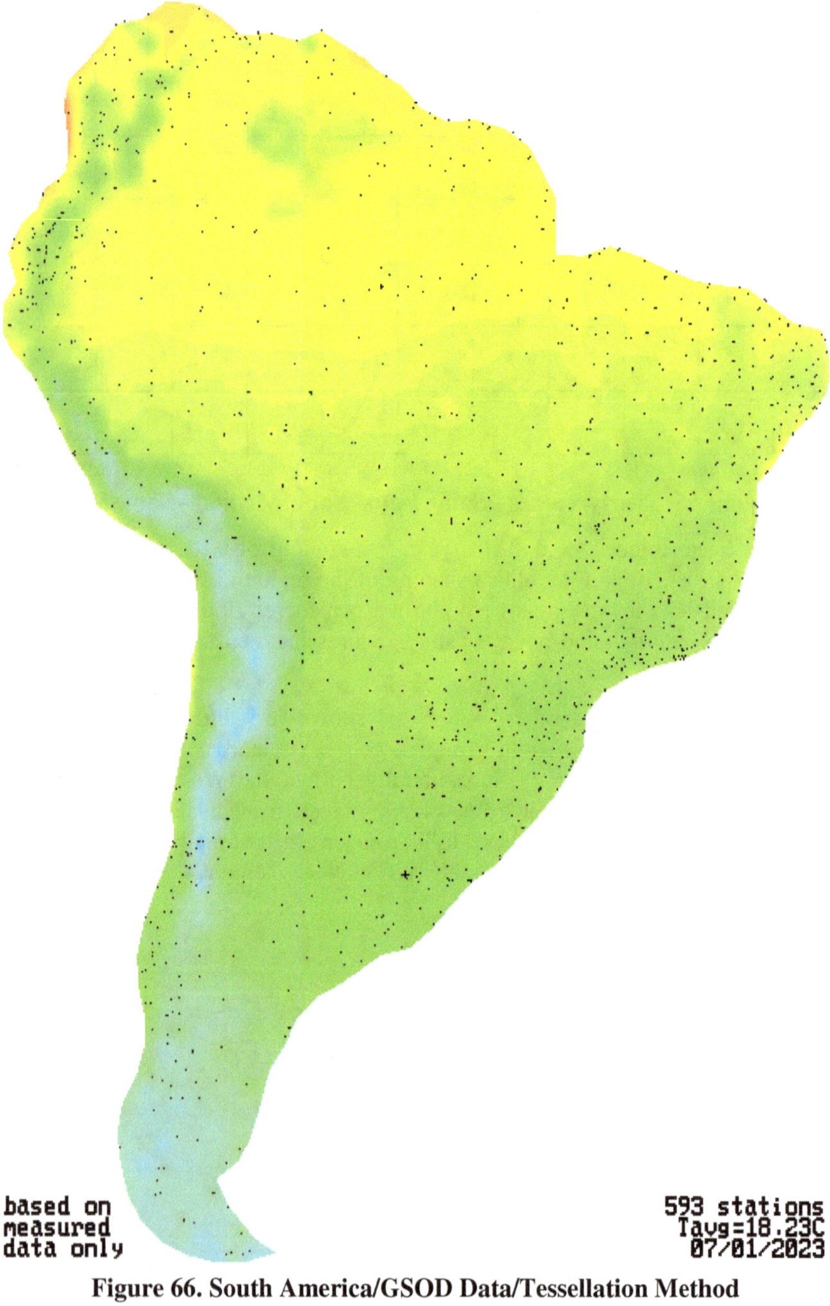

Figure 66. South America/GSOD Data/Tessellation Method

46

Aside from a little strip of heat in the northwest corner and a much longer one along the Andes, there's not much happening here either. The monthly averages are shown in this next figure:

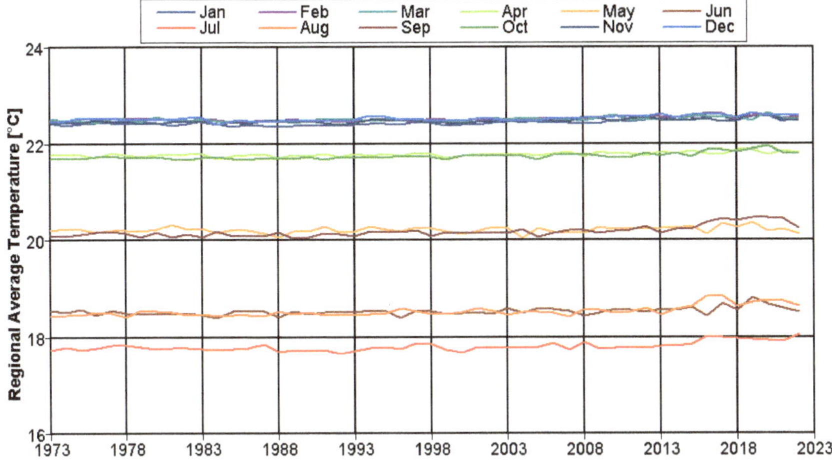

Figure 67. South America Avg. Temps. GSOD/Tess. Method

These trends are very similar to those of the Lower 48. The yearly values are shown next:

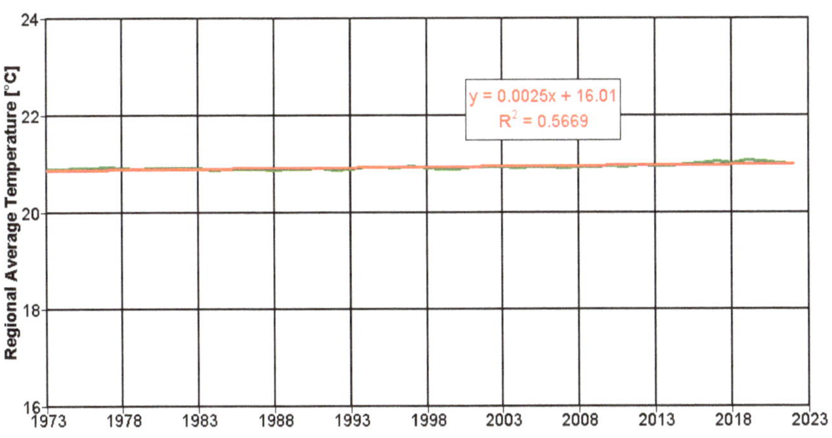

Figure 68. Yearly Values - Same Data - Same Method - Same Scale

The linear trend is +0.0025 °C/year or a miniscule warming rate of 0.25 °C/century. No cause for alarm here—at least for global warming. Clearly, there is reason for concern with deforestation, but you can't see that from looking at temperatures alone.

As we saw in the NASA "anomaly" map, the climate over most of the continent of Africa has also been fairly uniform, as illustrated below:

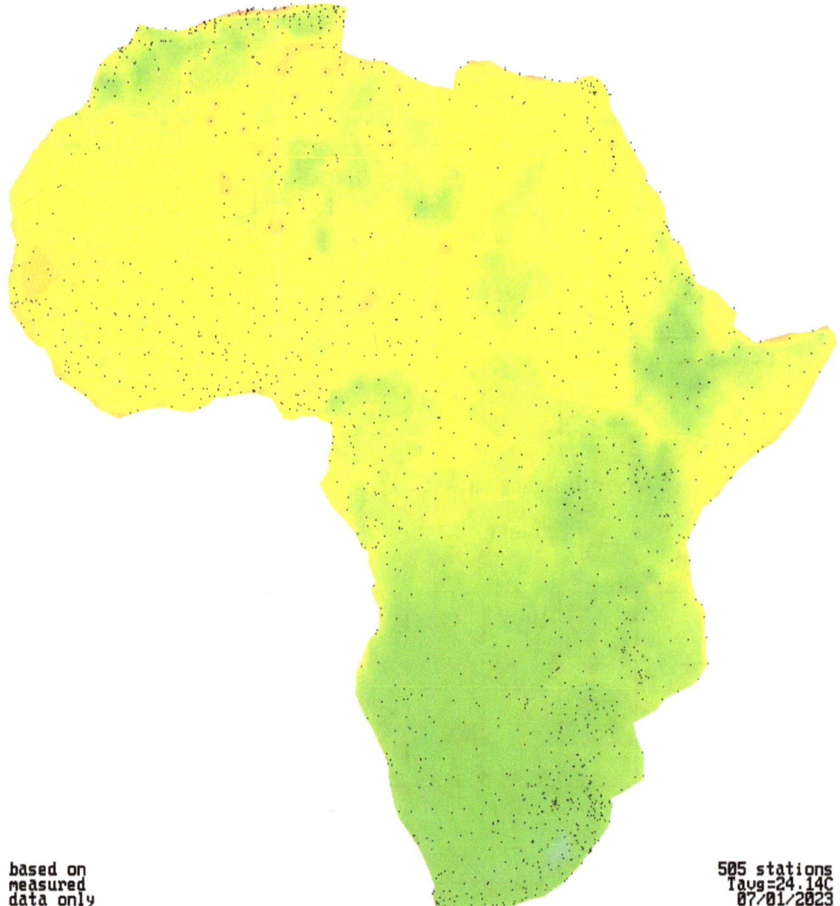

Figure 69. Africa/GSOD Data/Tessellation Method

We step through all of the GSOD collection, creating these maps and adding the results to the spreadsheet.

The resulting average monthly temperatures are:

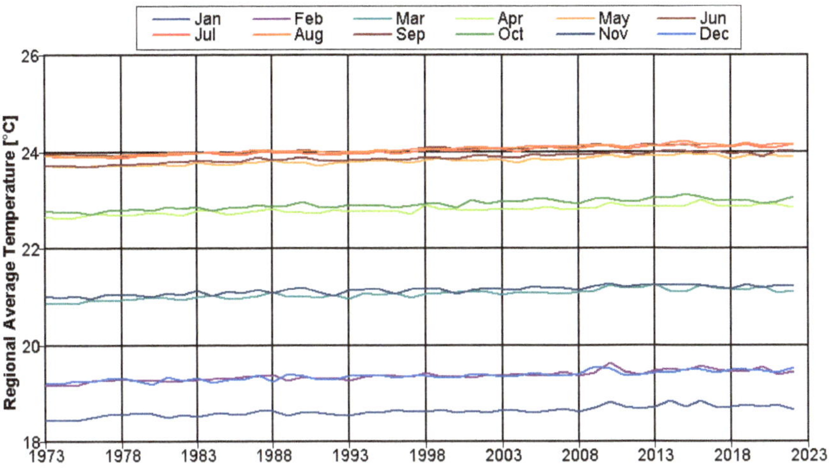

Figure 70. Africa Avg. Temps. GSOD/Tess. Method

And the yearly averages:

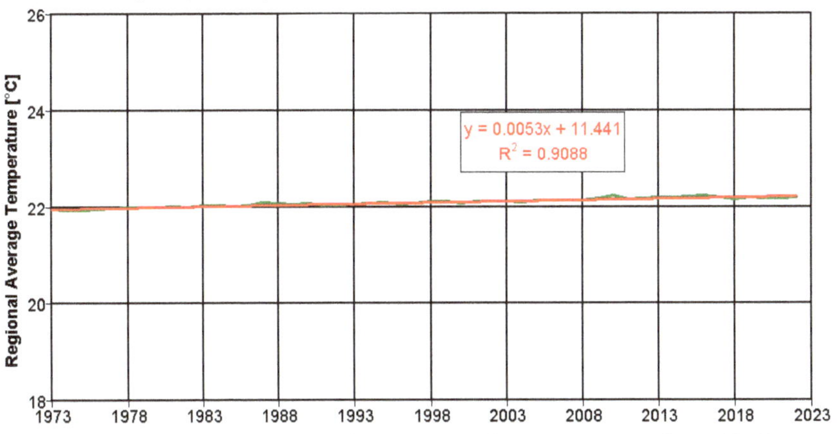

Figure 71. Yearly Values - Same Data - Same Method - Same Scale

The linear trend is +0.0053 °C/year or a tiny warming rate of 0.53 °C/century, roughly twice that of South America. This is also consistent with the NASA "anomaly" map. There has been much talk of "reparations" for Africa at recent climate change summits. There isn't much "global warming" or any sort of "climate change" so far as temperature happening in Africa to warrant this concern or proposed gesture.

One area of red on the NASA map is the Middle East and so we next consider that region, again using the same database (GSOD) and applying the same methodology (tessellation and solving Laplace's equation). July 1, 2023:

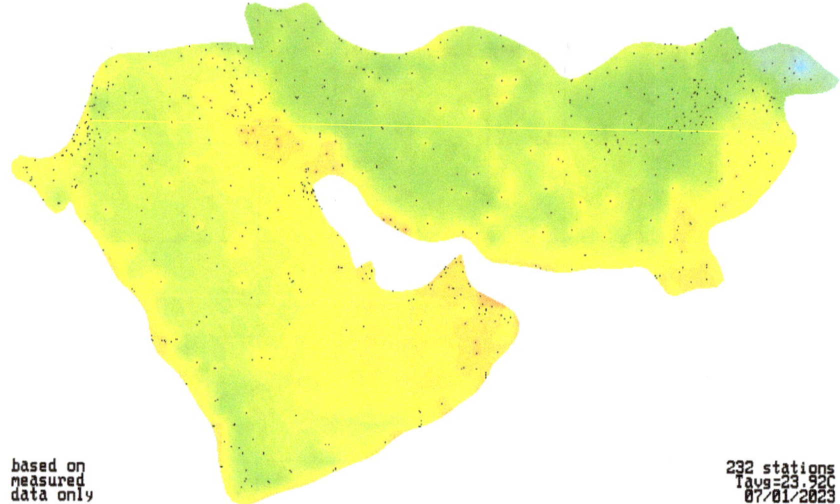

Figure 72. Middle East/GSOD Data/Tessellation Method

Not surprisingly, we see a little more heat in this map. We also see blue in the eastern region at high altitude. We will discuss the impact of altitude in the next chapter. The monthly average temperatures for this region are shown here:

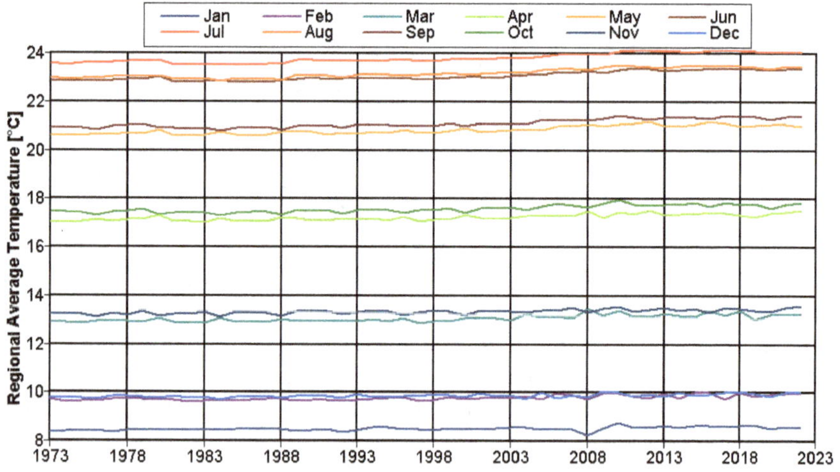

Figure 73. Middle East Avg. Temps. GSOD/Tess. Method

And the yearly ones here:

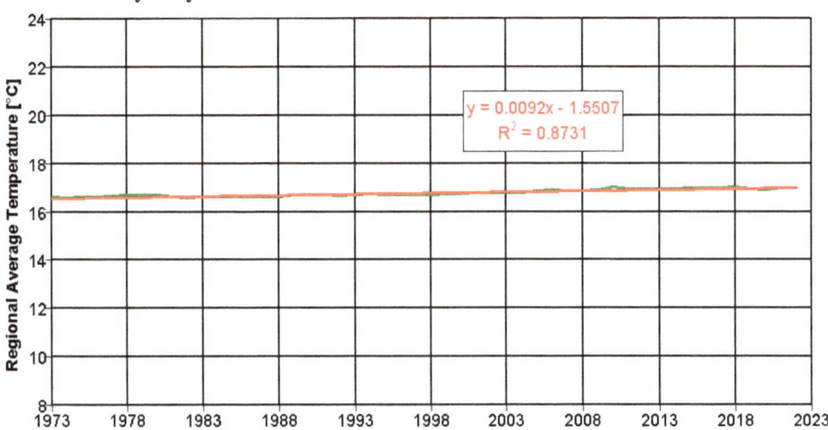

Figure 74. Yearly Values - Same Data - Same Method - Same Scale

The linear trend is +0.0092 °C/year or warming rate of 0.92 °C/century. Finally, we are seeing something near the much-touted 1.5 °C/century filling the headlines. This too is consistent with the NASA "anomaly" map. The people in this region have some reason to be concerned, but perhaps not quite as much as the western media might like to think because the weather has always been harsh and warm there.

Asia is a very large and diverse area populated by many different people and spans a wide range of industrialization. Here we see one day using the same data set (GSOD) and methodology (tessellation and solution of Laplace's equation):

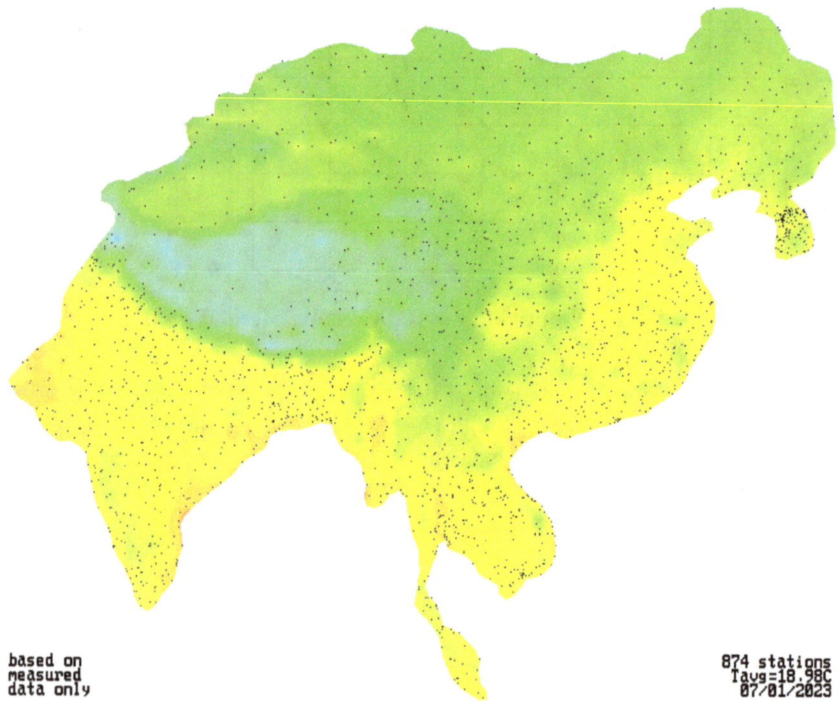

Figure 75. Asia/GSOD Data/Tessellation Method

The highest elevations on Earth (Himalayas) are within this area (which we have accounted for, as described in the next chapter). The monthly average temperatures are shown next:

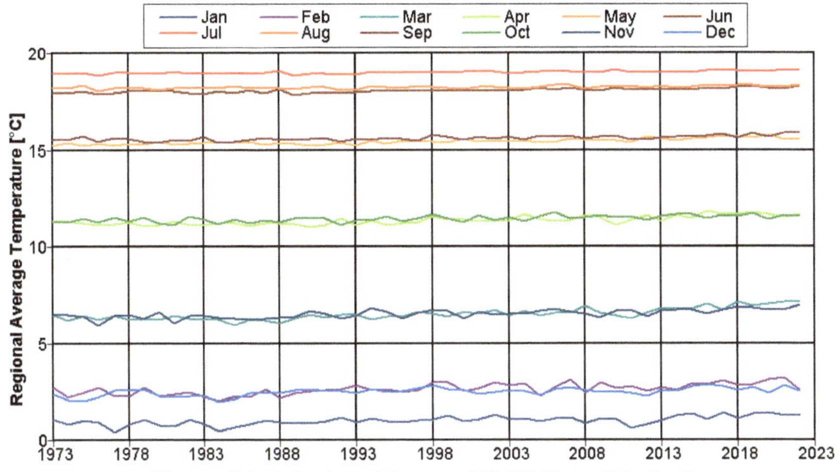

Figure 76. Asia Avg. Temps. GSOD/Tess. Method

And the yearly averages...

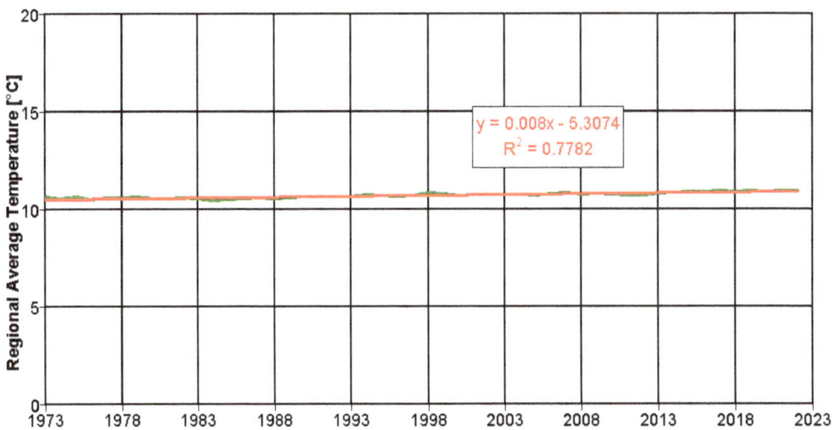

Figure 77. Yearly Values - Same Data - Same Method - Same Scale

The linear trend is +0.008 °C/year or warming rate of 0.8 °C/century. As for the Middle East, this slope is near the often-cited 1.5 °C/century. This is also consistent with the NASA "anomaly" map. The people in this region likely have some more cause for concern than those in the Middle East.

<u>British Isles</u>

Before we get to continental Europe, we focus on England, Ireland, Scotland, and Wales, where the masses bitterly weep that their children will never again play in the snow.

Figure 78. British Isles/GSOD Data/Tessellation Method

The regional average monthly temperatures using the same methodology:

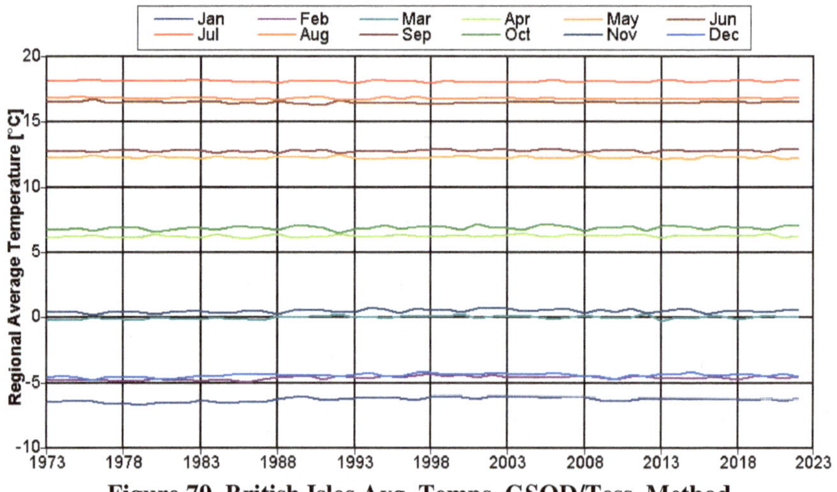

Figure 79. British Isles Avg. Temps. GSOD/Tess. Method

The yearly values are shown in this next figure:

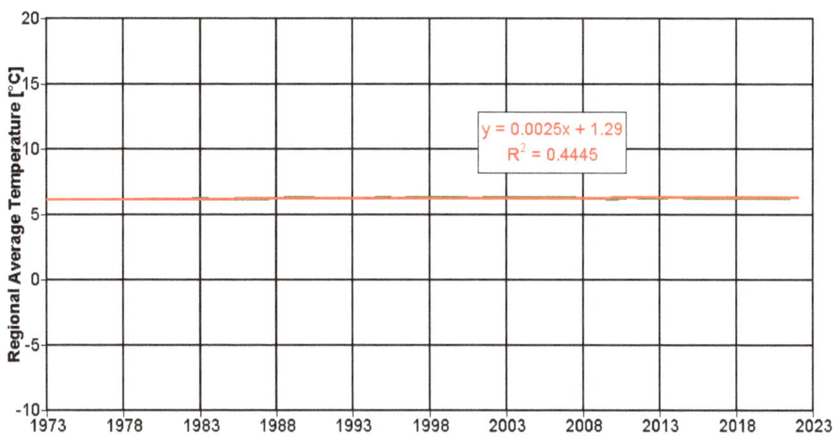

Figure 80. Yearly Values - Same Data - Same Method - Same Scale

The linear trend is +0.0025 °C/year or warming rate of 0.25 °C/century. Sorry... I'm just not feeling the pain here, Folks.

<u>Continental Europe</u>

At last, we get to the big bad dark red blob on the NASA Naughty List...

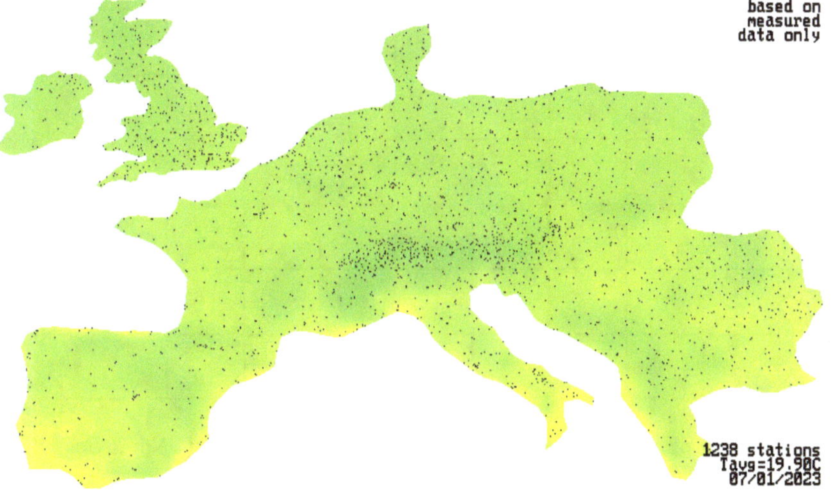

Figure 81. Europe/GSOD Data/Tessellation Method

We include the British Isles by proximity but exclude Scandinavia, as the climate is significantly different in that sub-region. The area of Continental Europe is larger and the climate more diverse than the British Isles alone.

Again, we apply the same methodology to arrive at average temperatures for the region:

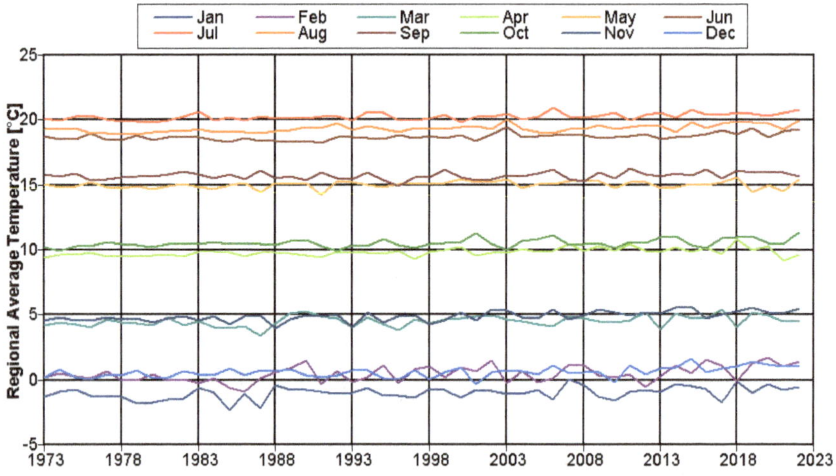

Figure 82. Europe Avg. Temps. GSOD/Tess. Method

And again for yearly values...

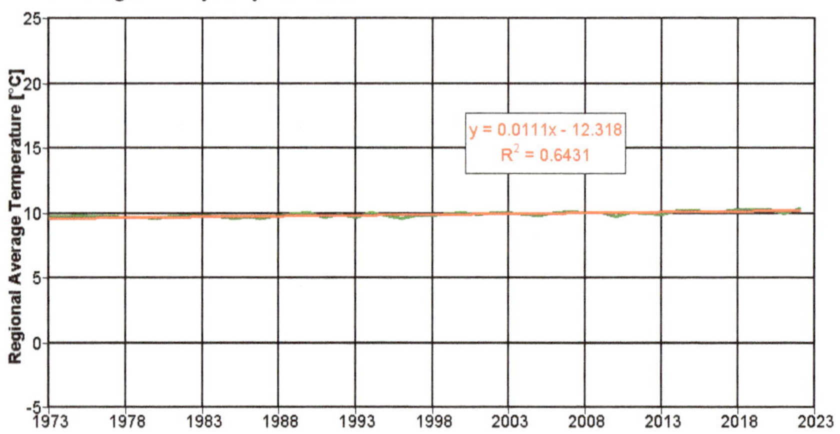

Figure 83. Yearly Values - Same Data - Same Method - Same Scale

The linear trend is +0.0111 °C/year or warming rate of 1.11 °C/century, again approaching the dreaded 1.5 °C/century slope. We have been careful to plot these yearly trends on the same scale as the monthly ones so as to avoid visual exaggeration, which might induce greater alarm than is warranted by the data.

The last region we will consider is Scandinavia. It is small and contributes little to the global picture but is of interest to many. Here we see temperatures for this same day of recent focus (7/1/2023):

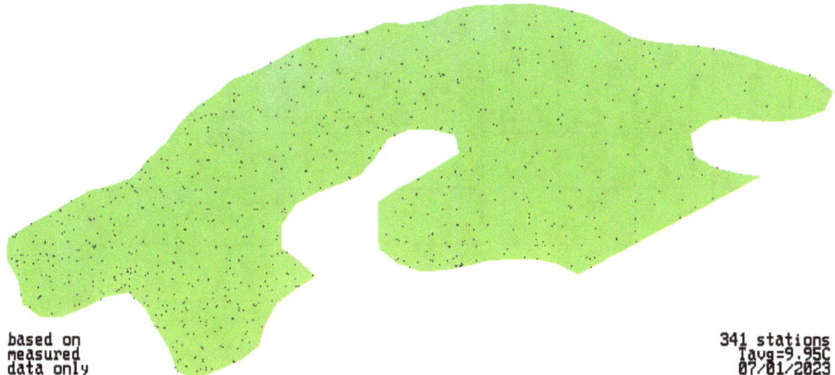

Figure 84. Scandinavia/GSOD Data/Tessellation Method

Note that I use the same temperature<>color scale regardless of the region. To do otherwise would be intentionally exaggerating local conditions, presumably to induce panic and hysteria. The average temperatures over this region by month are shown in this next figure:

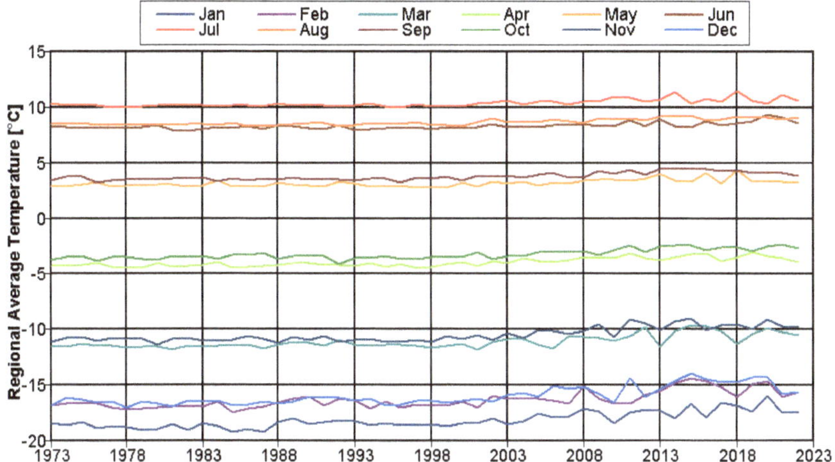

Figure 85. Scandinavia Avg. Temps. GSOD/Tess. Method

And again for yearly values...

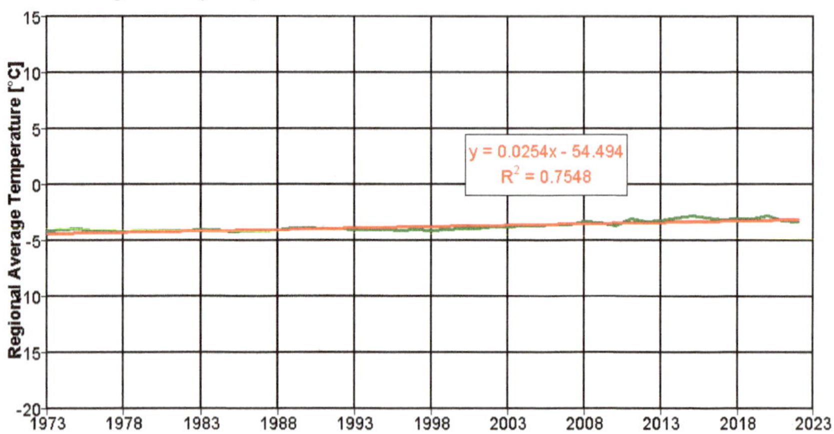

Figure 86. Yearly Values - Same Data - Same Method - Same Scale

The linear trend is +0.0254 °C/year or warming rate of 2.54 °C/century, more than twice that for the rest of Europe. This is consistent with the big dark red blob on the NASA Naughty List. It makes you wonder if perhaps somebody is burning a whole lot more fossil fuel than they are admitting. It's just a thought.

Chapter 7. Lapse Rate

Obviously, atmospheric temperature varies with elevation. We shouldn't merely average data from meteorological stations at low and high elevation, simply because they are nearby based solely on latitude and longitude.

Figure 87. Potential Locations for Meteorological Stations

According to the International Civil Aviation Organization, the standard (i.e., average, normal, typical) rate of decrease in air temperature with elevation is 6.49°C/km. They publish this value because it is of interest to pilots. While this is not always the case (there are temperature *inversions*) and this value may vary over space and with time, it's better than ignoring what is clearly a natural part of the meteorological data collected at stations all over the World.

The way we compensate for lapse rate is to subtract this from the temperature data (based on the elevation of the station, which is supplied along with the latitude and longitude) before combining it (regardless of the algorithm used (e.g., inverse distance, kriging, or solving Laplace's equation)) and then add it back based on the local (i.e., node) elevation. While the station locations are scattered about with varying density, elevation data are available at much more convenient intervals and accuracy.

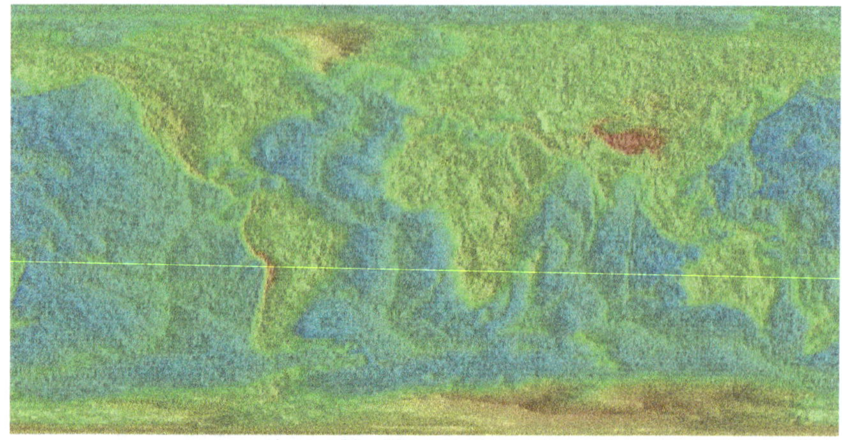

Figure 88. Global Topography

The first step implementing any of these temperature distributing and averaging algorithms is to create an elevation map corresponding to the grid:

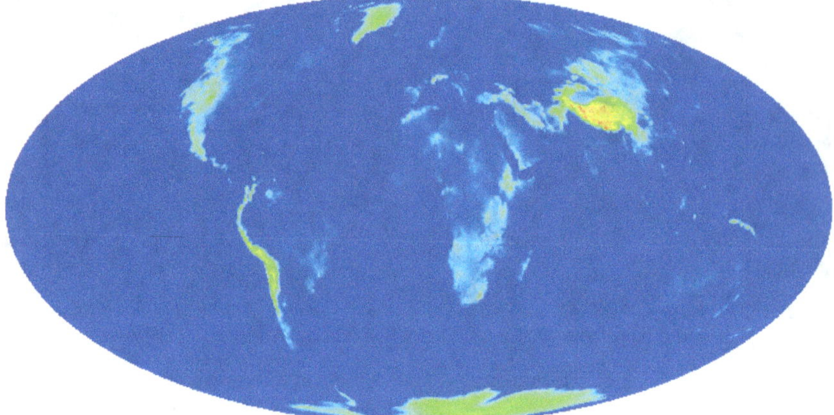

Figure 89. Elevations Mapped to Nodes Then to Projection

Chapter 8. Precipitation

All three of the data collections discussed herein contain precipitation data. We will only consider rain (liquid precipitation) and not snow fall or snow accumulation, as this information is much more sparse. There is no compelling reason why we shouldn't utilize the same calculations for rain. While there might be different forces of nature at work, we have no additional information with which to analyze the data available. We are accustomed to seeing rain visually depicted differently than temperature; therefore, we modify the "painting" process but not the number crunching.

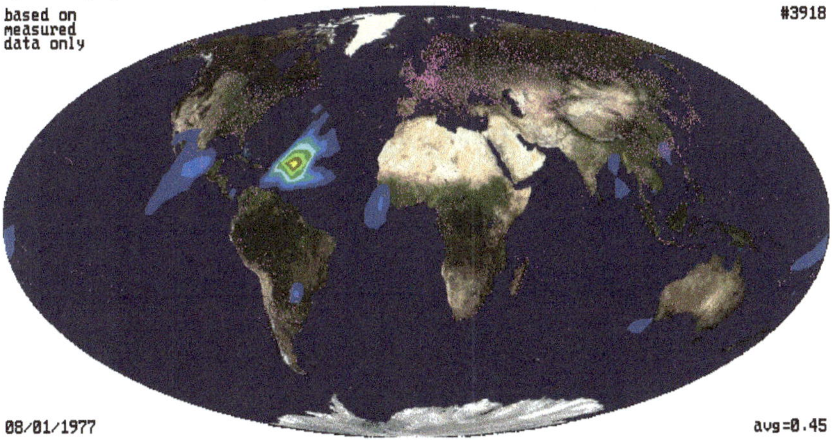

Figure 90. Global Rain Contours

The magenta specks are the stations reporting precipitation. This particular frame shows hurricane Anita. This next figure shows the Typhoon of 1975:

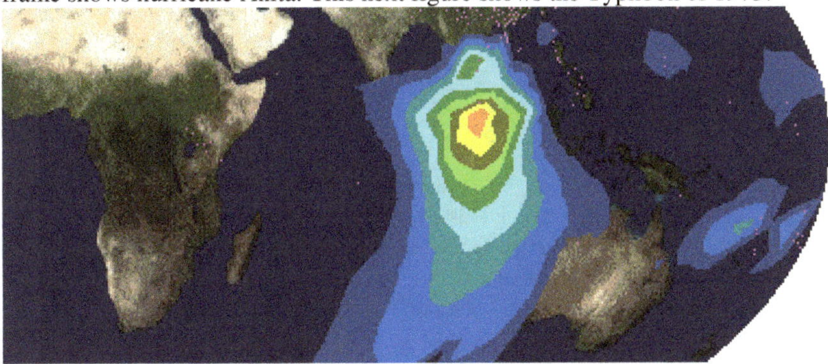

Figure 91. Typhoon 1975

We can process the GSOD collection, only for precipitation to arrive at global average values. The monthly averages are shown in this next figure:

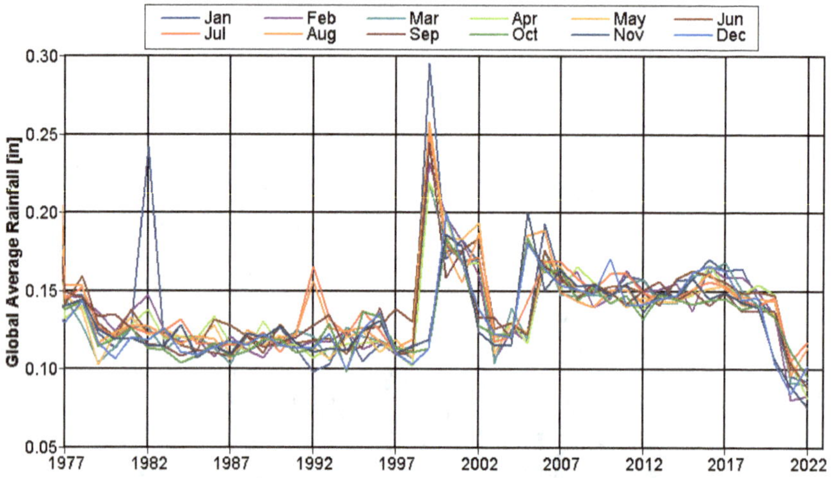

Figure 92. Global Average Rainfall Based on GSOD+Laplace by Month

And the yearly average:

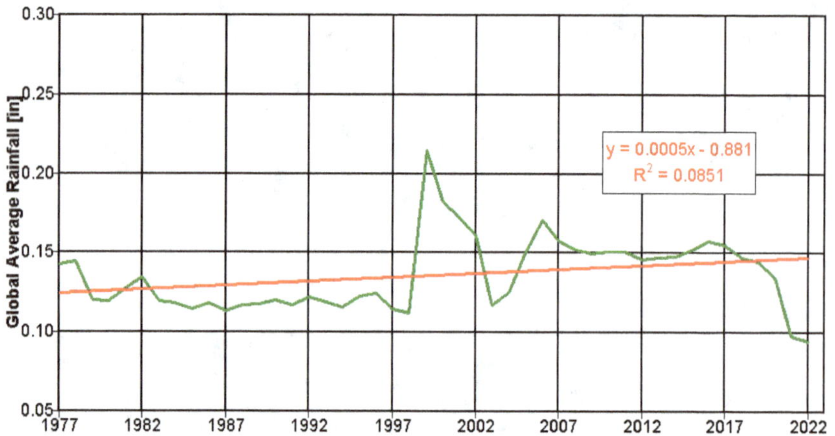

Figure 93. Yearly Values - Same Data - Same Method - Same Scale

There would appear to be a slight increasing trend in rainfall, though something strange began around 2020. Something strange happened in 1999, 2003, and 2006 too, so it's hard to tell. Precipitation data are not as complete as temperature with only about one-fifth as many stations reporting; so we must consider this trend more tentative than any of the temperature trends.

In spite of there being far less (1/5th) the data to work with and no meaningful discussion of the known discrepancies between measured rainfall and how much actually ends up in rivers and lakes (e.g., the experience with TVA's reservoirs), alarming maps of rainfall deficit still appear in the news. We can begin with the GSOD data, calculate a trend for each station, and then map the trends over the surface of the Earth to obtain the following map:

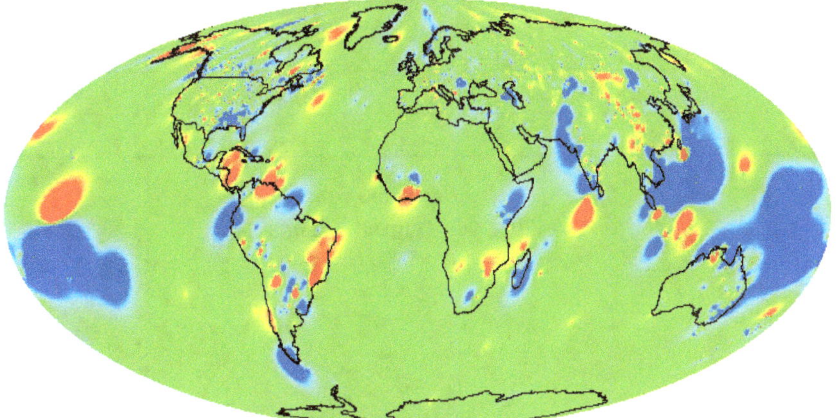

Figure 94. Station Rainfall Trends (not Rainfall)

Note that plotting the trend is not the same as plotting the data. For example, the data may vary considerably, yet the trend shows up as flat... or the other way around. Re-coloring this same information in NASA's scary palette:

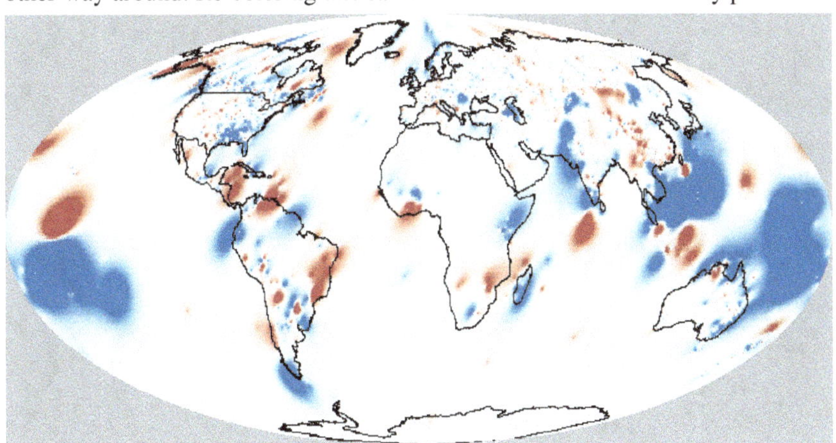

Figure 95. Same Data with Scary Palette

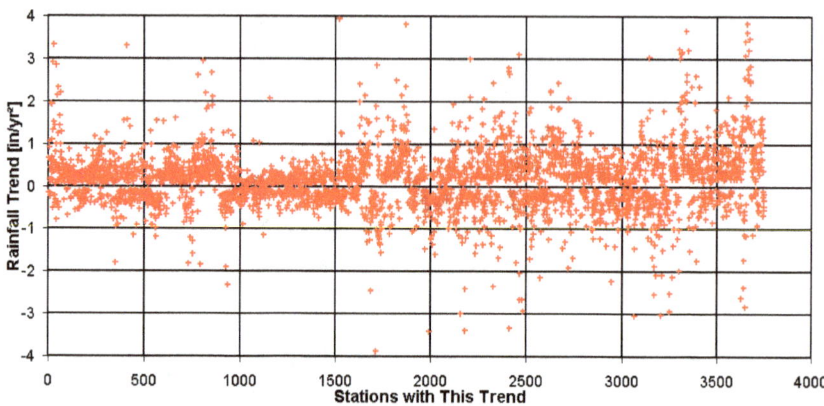

Figure 96. Rainfall Trends

Chapter 9. Humidity

Humidity is distinct from rainfall and is typically measured via the dew point, which is the temperature at which condensation begins to form. Dew point is easily measured and the instruments require little maintenance (especially when compared to a wet bulb device, which is the next most common measurement). We calculate the relative humidity or the percentage of the maximum water vapor bearing capacity of the air at a given condition (temperature and pressure). This calculation can be found on the Web and free software to implement such calculations can be found at the address beneath the Preface.

We distribute humidity data over the Globe exactly as for temperature and precipitation, using the same database and algorithms. We paint humidity as for rain, which is somewhat more familiar graphically. A typical day is shown in this first figure:

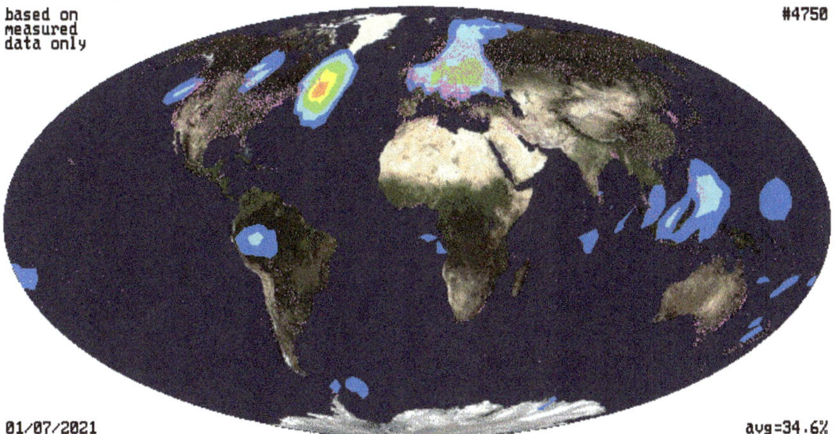

Figure 97. Global Relative Humidity

In this manner (i.e., global tessellation and solution of Laplace's equation) we can process the collection from 1973 to the present (i.e., the span having the most data). The global average humidity for each month is shown in this next figure:

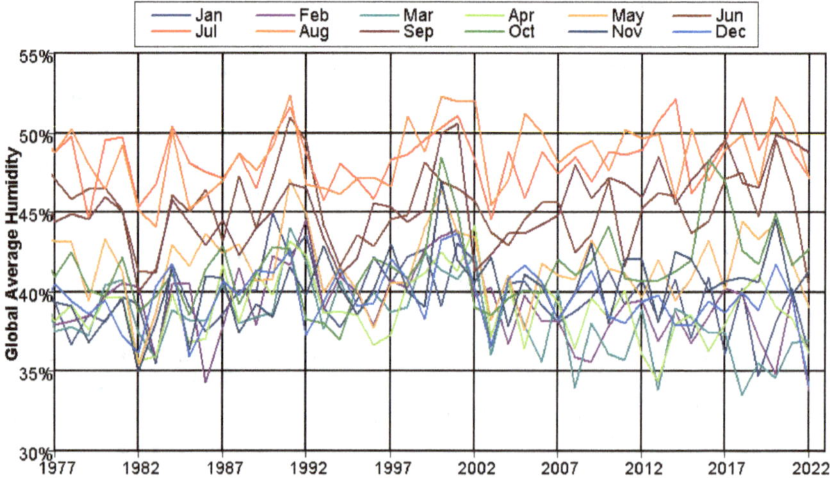

Figure 98. Monthly Values of Global Average Relative Humidity

The yearly values are also calculated and graphed as before (i.e., on the same scale so as to not intentionally exaggerate):

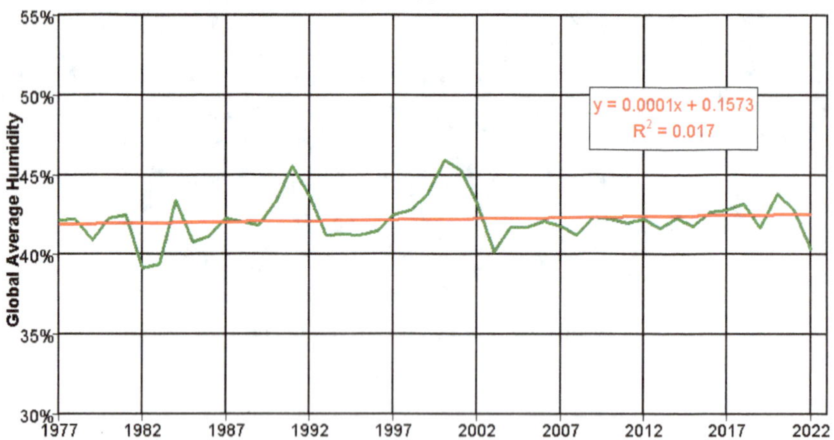

Figure 99. Yearly Values - Same Data - Same Method - Same Scale

Again, I'm not sure what the trend might mean...

Chapter 10. Barometric Pressure

Before the age of constant weather forecasts broadcast for all to hear, the barometer was often the indicator of weather to come. Decorative barometers such as this were often hung on the wall.

Figure 100. Decorative Barometer

Observations over many years inspired some generalities, including:

1) high barometric pressure usually means fair (i.e., good) weather
2) low barometric pressure usually means foul (i.e., bad) weather
3) rising pressure usually means improving weather
4) falling pressure usually means foul weather's coming

Over the years barometers have come in many shapes and utilized more than one principle or mechanism. A few are illustrated below:

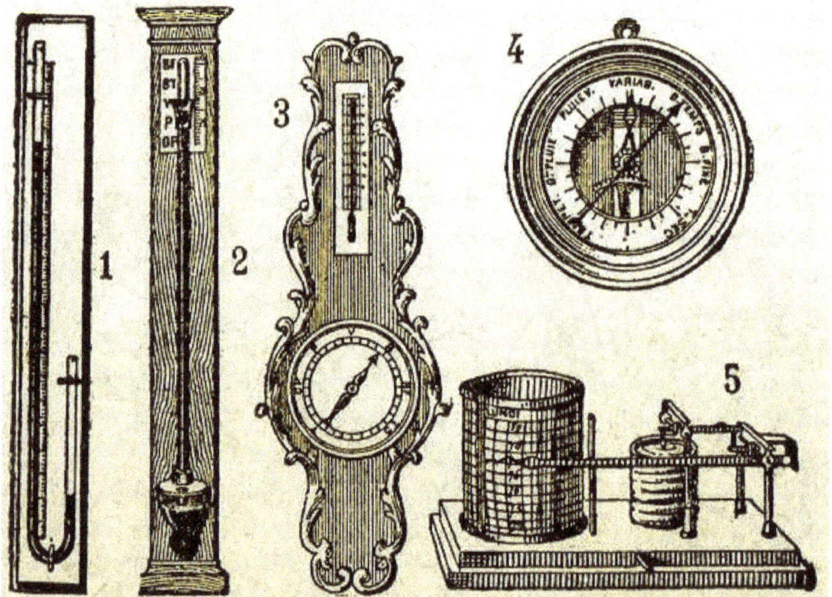

Figure 101. Antique Barometers (credit: Thomaston Collection)

As discussed in Chapter 1, stations may report STP (local station pressure at elevation) and/or SLP (pressure adjusted to sea level). We also discussed the difficulty and ambiguity of converting from one to the other. We further suspect that not every station (or agency) in every country performs this calculation in the same way or even describes what they are doing consistently. Barometric pressure data, therefore, has a similar tentative nature as does precipitation.

Still, we can and have analyzed it in the same way. Instead of painting the Globe in a rainbow, as for temperatures, or painting colorful blobs, as for rain and humidity, we draw contours of constant barometric pressure, as illustrated below:

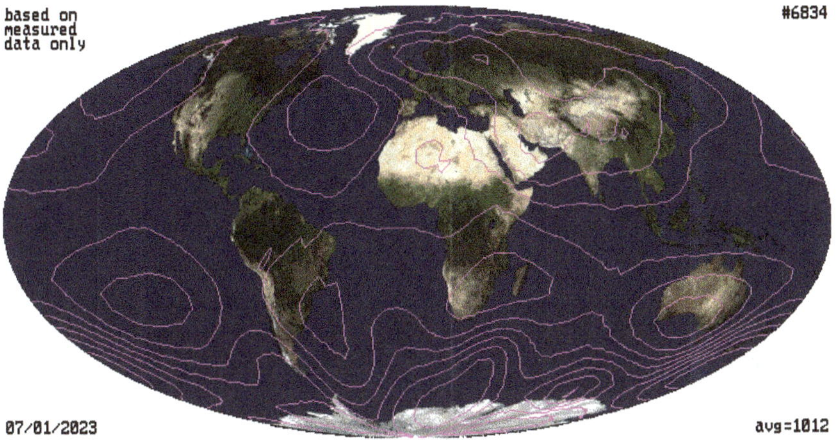

Figure 102. Global Barometric Pressure Contours

The global average barometric pressure by month is shown in this next figure:

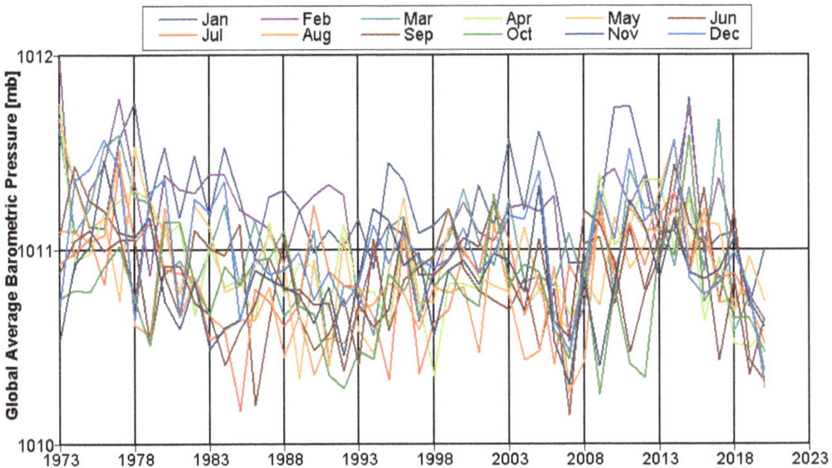

Figure 103. Global Average Barometric Pressure by Month

The yearly values are:

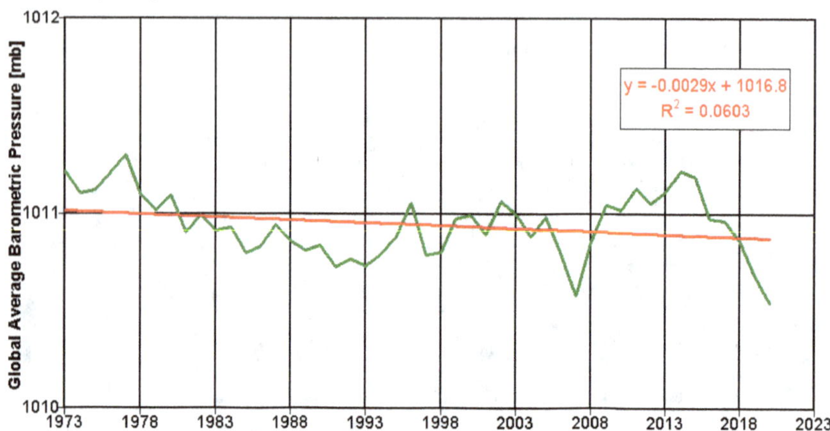

Figure 104. Yearly Values - Same Data - Same Method - Same Scale

I'm not sure what a "trend" upward or downward in average barometric pressure would mean. The Earth is probably not "losing" or "creating" more air. The total barometric pressure over the entire Globe must equal the total weight of air. Of course, this does include a considerable amount of moisture (i.e., water vapor) and perhaps that is on the way up or down.

Chapter 11. Wind

The main reason we bother calculating the distribution of pressure over the Earth and why we paint contours of constant barometric pressure (i.e., isobars) is so that we can take the gradient of these and calculate wind. The *gradient* is a common operation in differential calculus. There are many articles on the Web devoted to this subject. In three-dimensional Cartesian coordinates the gradient is defined:

$$\nabla p = \frac{\partial p}{\partial x}\,\hat{i} + \frac{\partial p}{\partial y}\,\hat{j} + \frac{\partial p}{\partial x}\,\hat{k} \tag{11.1}$$

The pressure, p, is a scalar but the gradient (∇p) is a vector. The three spatial components are indicated by the three unit vectors ($\hat{i}$, $\hat{j}$, $\hat{k}$). The wind speed and direction is proportional to and in line with the negative of the gradient of the barometric pressure. The constant of proportionality can be calculated from measured wind speeds. For example, these contours:

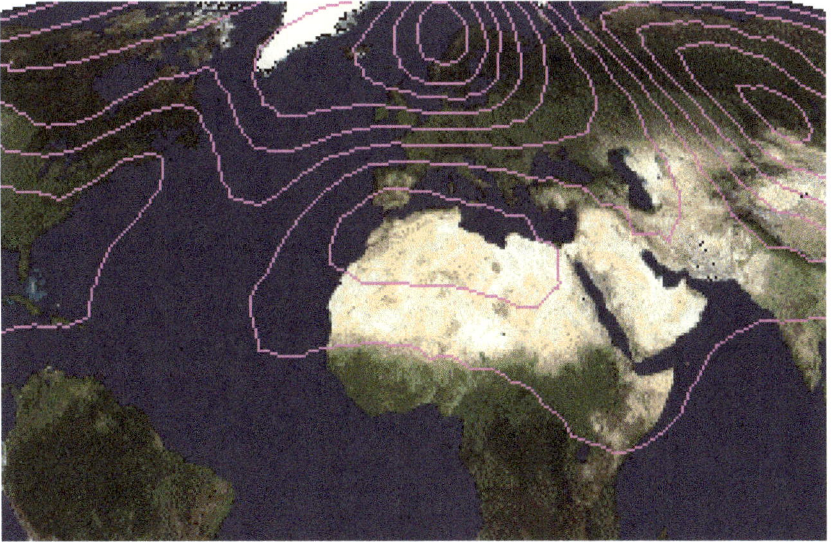

Figure 105. Barometric Pressure Contours

Result in these wind vectors:

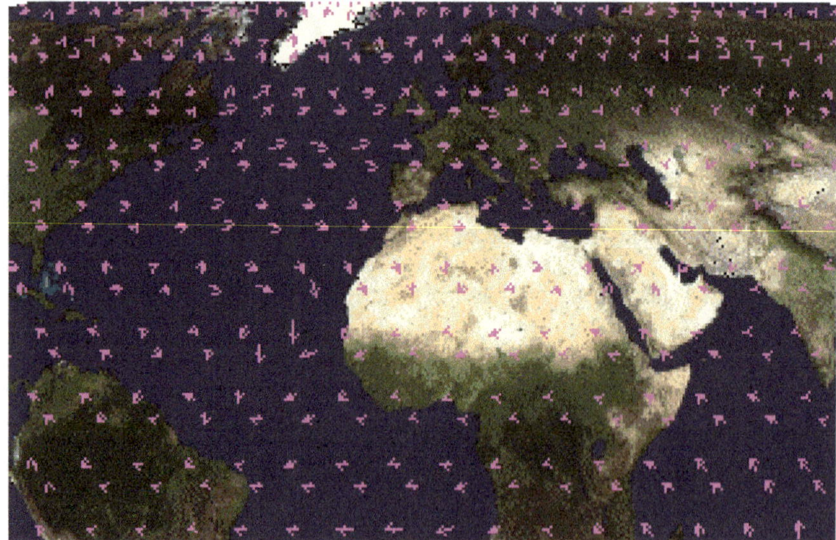

Figure 106. Wind Vectors

This map is for 1/1/1973, the beginning of the more complete part of the GSOD collection:

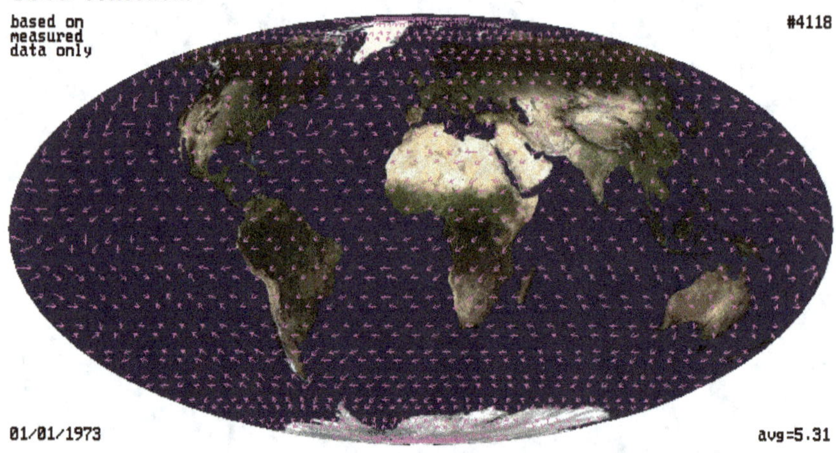

Figure 107. Global Wind Vectors for 1/1/1973

Most of the bulk meteorological collections contain barometric pressure but not all contain wind. Even the ones which do contain wind often don't include the direction, making it difficult to utilize this information. If barometric pressure is provided, then wind vectors can be calculated (estimated). The GSOD collection does include both (barometric pressure and wind speed);

therefore, we can calculate the constant of proportionality in knots per millibar per meter. Wind is usually reported in knots. One knot is approximately 1.151 mph or 0.514 m/s. Barometric pressure is usually reported in millibar and the tessellated grid is based on the radius of the Earth in meters, which works into calculation of the gradient.

This map is for 7/1/2023

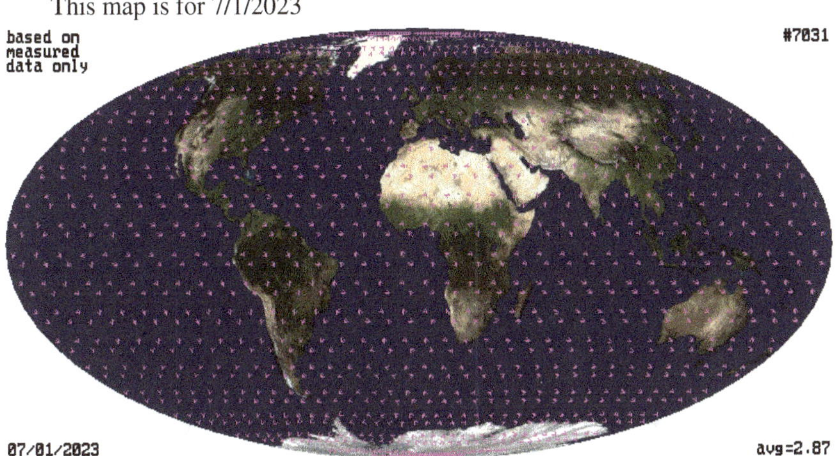

Figure 108. Global Wind Vectors for 7/1/2023

Using this approach (tessellated sphere, solve Laplace's equation to get barometric pressure over the entire surface of the Earth, take the gradient to get wind speed and direction) we can process the GSOD collection from 1973 to the present. The global average monthly winds are found to be:

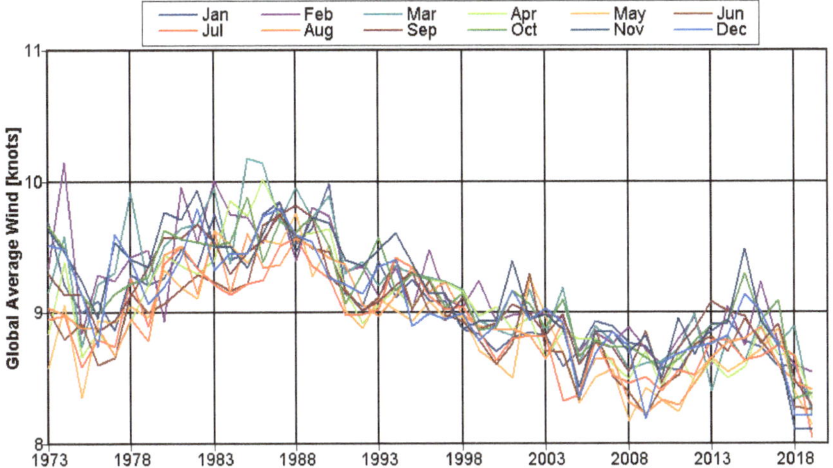

Figure 109. Global Average Wind by Month (Baro+Laplace+Gradient)

The yearly averages are shown in this next figure:

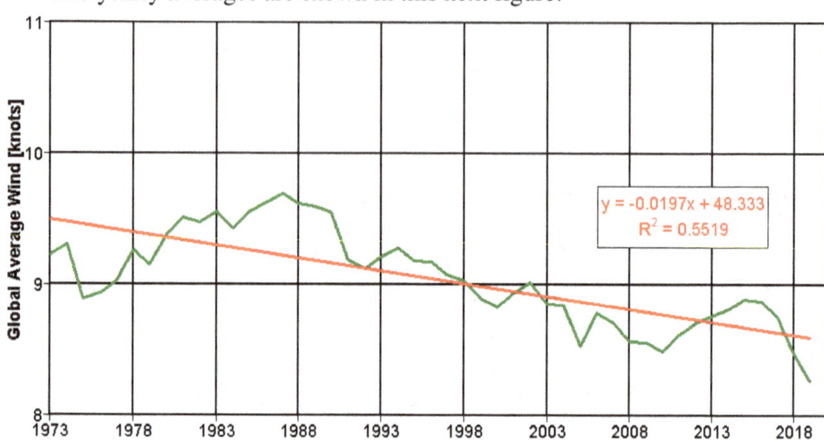

Figure 110. Yearly Values - Same Data - Same Method - Same Scale

I'm not sure what the trend means, whether the World is getting calmer (less windy) or the data is being reported more consistently. It's hard to tell, especially with pressure data when there is a lack of consistency calculating sea level pressure from station pressure.

Chapter 12. Records

There is much ado about climate records; that is, record hottest and coldest days. To be sure, there is some record broken somewhere on the face of the Earth every day. The big question is: are these occurring more often and what does it mean? There are two big challenges to this narrative, which we shall address before examining the data. 1) There are more meteorological stations being set up and collecting data all the time, so there are naturally more record highs and lows being set at these increasingly newer stations. 2) The environment surrounding many older meteorological stations is changing due to urbanization so that comparing data from a station that was once in the woods or a suburb to more recent data when that same station has become surrounded by urban sprawl is not a fair comparison. This is addition to the ongoing concern that many meteorological stations are located at in airport—right in the middle of an asphalt heat dish were aircraft jet engines belch out hot air throughout the day and night.

Let us first consider some long-term stations by themselves. The first of these is Knoxville, Tennessee.

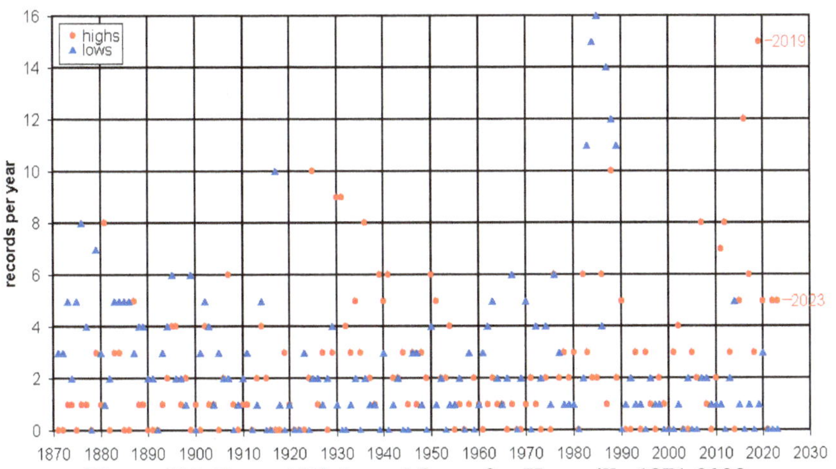

Figure 111. Record Highs and Lows for Knoxville 1871-2023

There were quite a few highs from 1925 to 1941 and even more lows between 1983 and 1989. There were more highs in 2019 than any year but fewer in 2022, which matched 2020 and 1990 before that and 1951 before that and 1932 before that and so on.

Here are the monthly average temperatures for this same site:

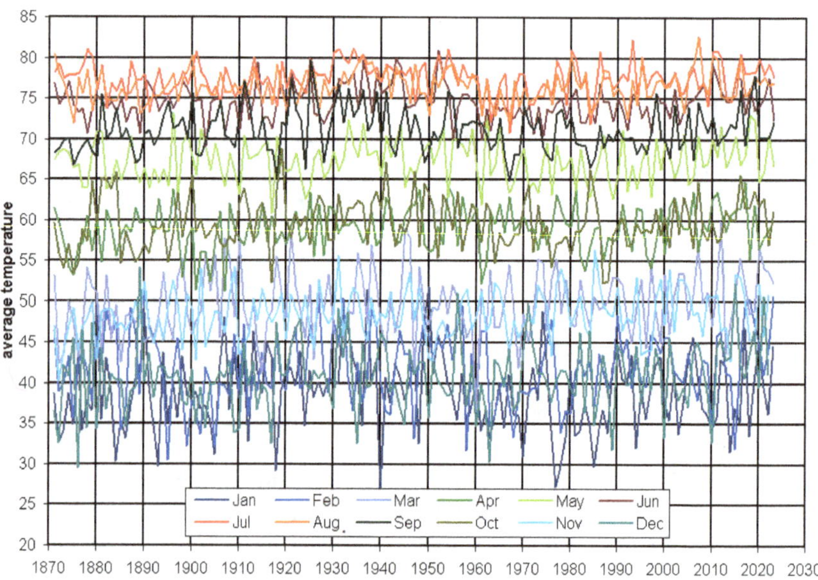

Figure 112. Monthly Average Temperature for Knoxville 1871-2023

Perhaps this city is an anomaly. After all, it lies within the bounds of the Tennessee Valley Authority, which has long been committed to protecting the environment. We next consider a coastal city: Charleston, South Carolina:

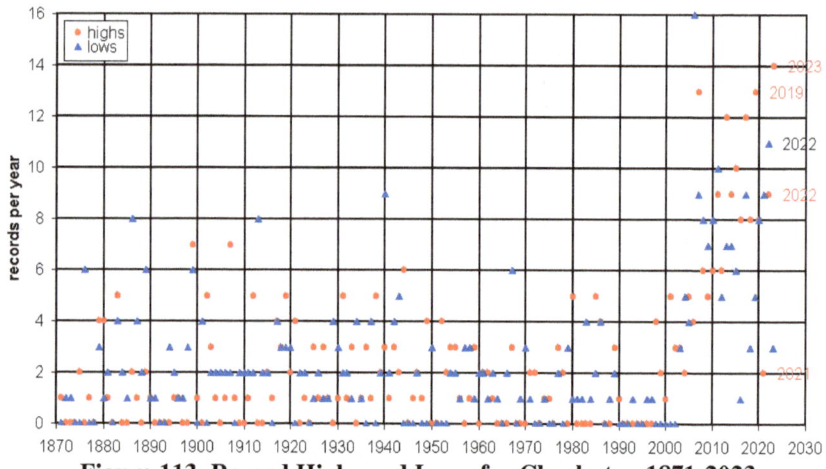

Figure 113. Record Highs and Lows for Charleston 1871-2023

Here we see what looks like a trend to more highs (and lows) approaching the present. 2023 has the most highs with 2019 a close second but 2022 had the same number of highs as 2011 and 2014 plus 2021 was way down with 2004 and 1875. 2013 saw many highs but 2012 and 2014 didn't. If you want to see a pattern in this data, you probably will. If you choose to see a hockey stick in the middle of this graph, focusing only on the red and ignoring the blue spots and 2021, which doesn't fit the pattern, that's your choice; but please don't demand that see one too or vilify me for disagreeing with you.

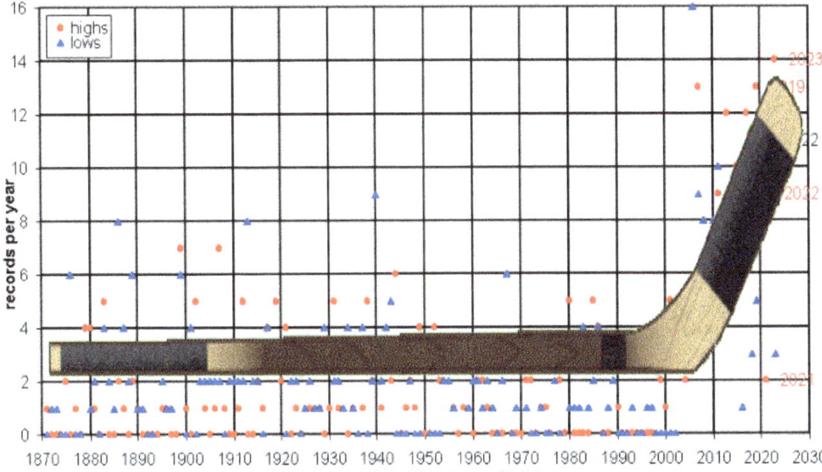

Figure 114. Hockey Stick

Here are the monthly average temperatures for Charleston:

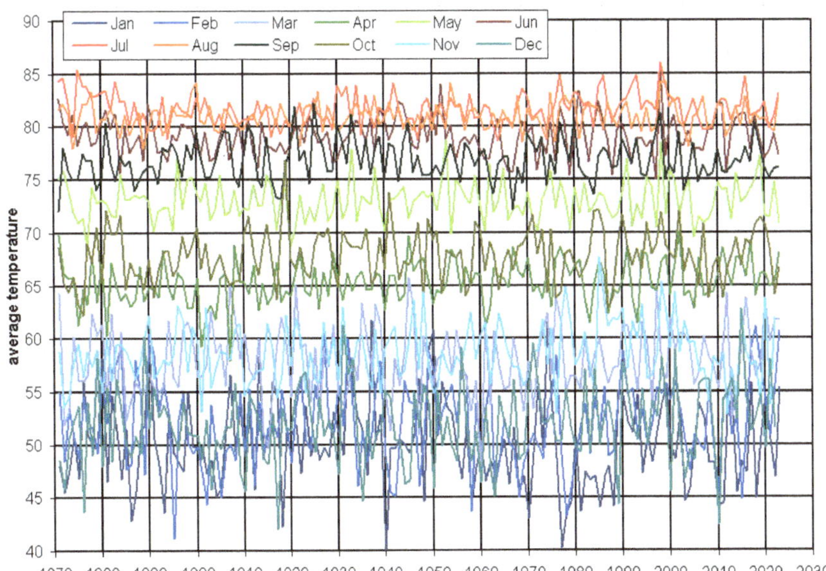

Figure 115. Monthly Average Temperature for Charleston 1871-2023

Well... maybe Knoxville, nestled as it is in the lush Tennessee Valley, is safe but those coastal towns are in big trouble... or are they? Let's look at Savannah, Georgia.

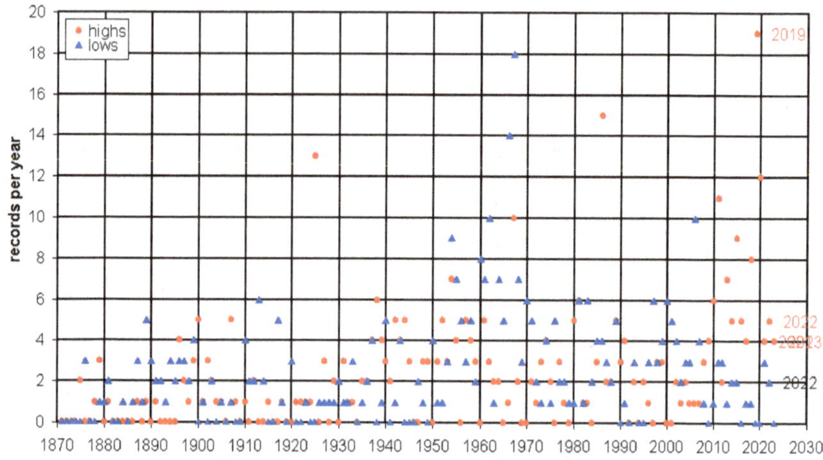

Figure 116. Record Highs and Lows for Savannah 1871-2023

It seems 2019 was a scorcher but wait... 2021, 2022, and 2023 are hiding down there next to 2009 and 2017. Up... down... down... up... down... down... like a rollercoaster. Let's just stick to the data...

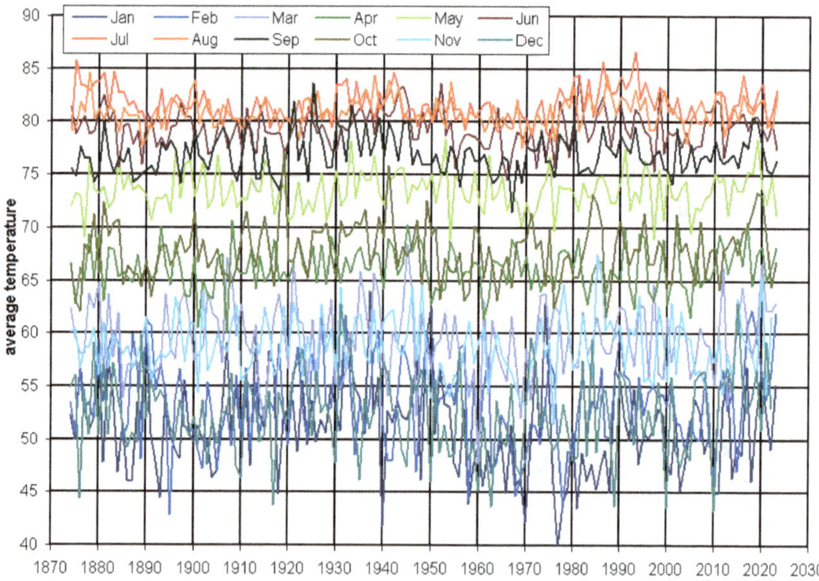

Figure 117. Monthly Average Temperature for Savannah 1871-2023

78

We could keep this up for a very long time, as I have this same span of data for hundreds of locations. We next turn to the USHCN/NDP-070 (Lower 48) Collection.

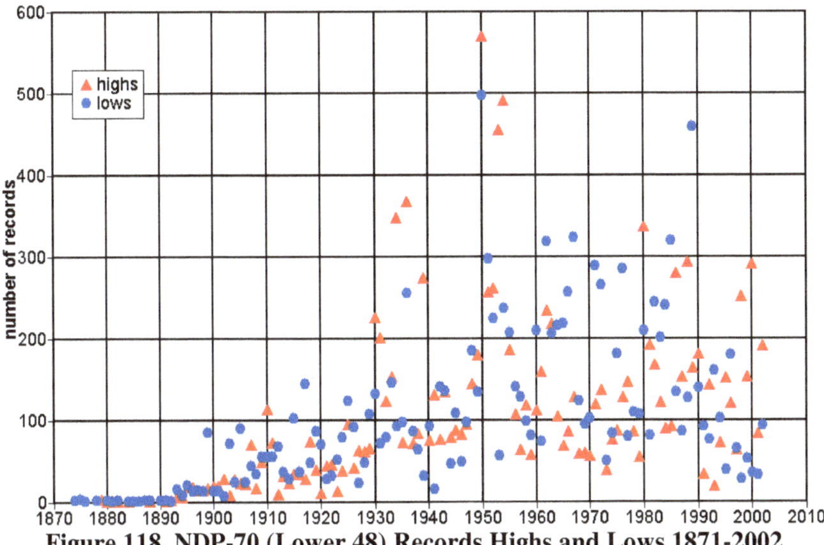

Figure 118. NDP-70 (Lower 48) Records Highs and Lows 1871-2002

Consider what this graph shows: If the record high for the month of June for a particular station over its entire period of record (i.e., 1871-2002) occurred in 1936, that would be 1 record in 1986. The most number of record highs (570) for this collection occurred in 1950. The most number of record lows (498) also occurred in this same year! And some people think the climate is getting more erratic? There understandably few record highs and lows in the early years because there were fewer stations reporting (see Figure 17), especially before 1931.

<u>Fallacy of Omission</u>

This might be a good point to mention a rarely discussed topic... You can communicate as much by what you choose not to say, as what you do say. This is called the *fallacy of omission*. If you only mention the data that supports your pet narrative, careful to always leave out the data that doesn't, this can be described as *cherry picking*. A more recent term is: *confirmation bias*. Notice that I have included several graphs that showed a global warming trend. Notice also the I included the Charleston data, which sort of, not really, fit the hockey stick pattern. I also included graphs that don't show a regional warming trend (e.g., Lower 48 and Australia) and ones that don't look like a hockey stick (e.g., Knoxville and Savannah).

79

We next consider the global collection (GSOD), which contains thousands of stations and extends back to 1929, though there were far fewer stations before 1973. The record highs and lows for this global database are shown in this next figure:

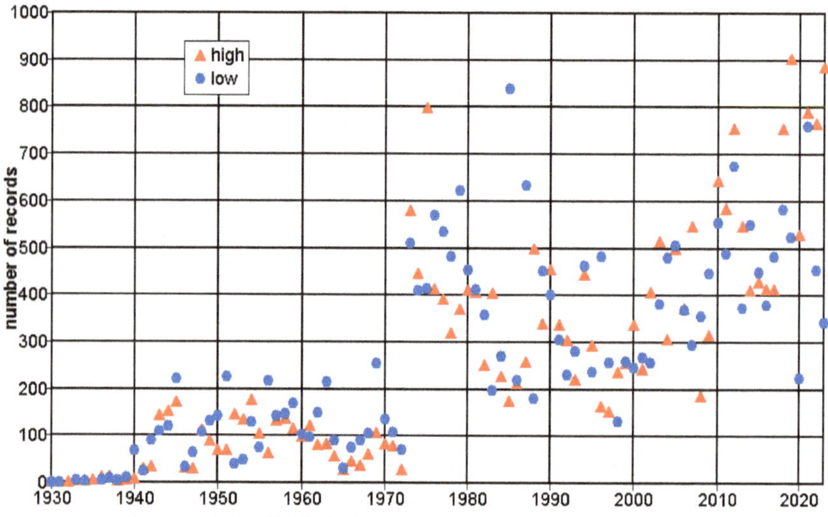

Figure 119. Global Record Highs and Lows (GSOD)

It is not surprising that there are more records after 1973 than before, so consider these two groups separately. First, what does this figure show? If the all-time record high (any day, any month) for a particular station occurred in 1974, then that's 1 record counted for 1974. There are more red triangles in the upper right corner of this graph than anywhere else but this only exhibits a "trend" if you ignore the changing number of stations and the data from 1975 to 1985. One might argue for an inverted horseshoe pattern but another hockey stick is debatable.

80

Consider the following image:

Figure 120. Duck or Rabbit?

I don't know what your answer is, but mine is: It could be either one. And that's exactly how I view this climate data. We do appear to be in a period of increase variability with some warmer, some colder, some wetter, and some dryer conditions. Is all of this due primarily to a single cause (i.e., increased CO_2 emissions)? Perhaps, but not likely—unless somebody isn't accurately reporting their emissions. Are we headed for Doomsday in the near future? No. I hope you do realize, based on the vast oil and gas deposits in the Middle East, that region was once a rain forest. Mammoths once thrived in Siberia. Was the climate much different in the past? Yes! Did the animals survive those conditions? A

Let's look at this same information (records in the GSOD collection):

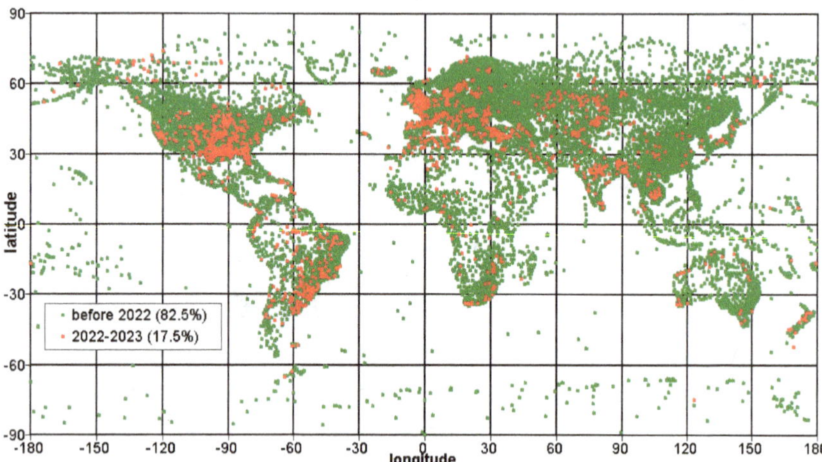

Figure 121. Same Data (GDOS Records) Different View

Every station with a record high in 2022 or 2023 is shown as red spots and those with record highs before 2022 are shown as green spots. In this presentation, it looks like records were set all over the US and Europe during this time and, in fact, they were! Before we jump of a bridge in despair, let's take another look at this same data.

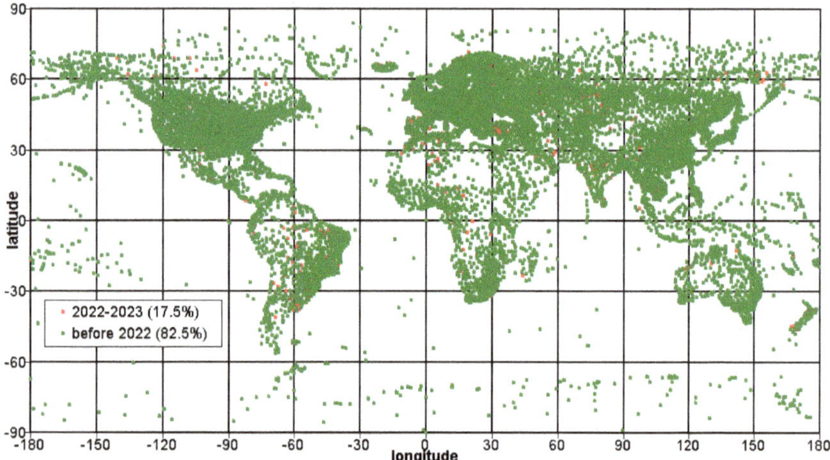

Figure 122. Exact Same Data but Red before Green

This is the same spreadsheet! The only difference is that the red spots are drawn first and then the green ones (note: series order swapped in the legend); whereas before the green ones were drawn before the red ones. The first figure

82

looks like Doomsday has arrived while the second looks like business as usual, but it's the exact same data and spreadsheet! The truth is somewhere between the two. This is another illustration of how (let's hope innocently) the same data can be presented and cause hysteria... or not.

We've already looked at the trend for the Lower 48, which is sprinkled with red dots in Figure 121 (see Figures 28, 29, 61, and 62). These clearly show a negligible long-term trend, neither warming nor cooling, yet Figure 121 would seem to indicate extreme warming. How do rational, reasonable people make sense of this? Carefully examine *all* of the data in more than one way (or view or graph) and cling to the facts. When it's not clear, keep an open mind. In the meanwhile, don't make a mess and clean up after yourself—cherish nature and protect it.

<u>Record Lows</u>

Before leaving this data set, we consider the record lows before 2022 and after:

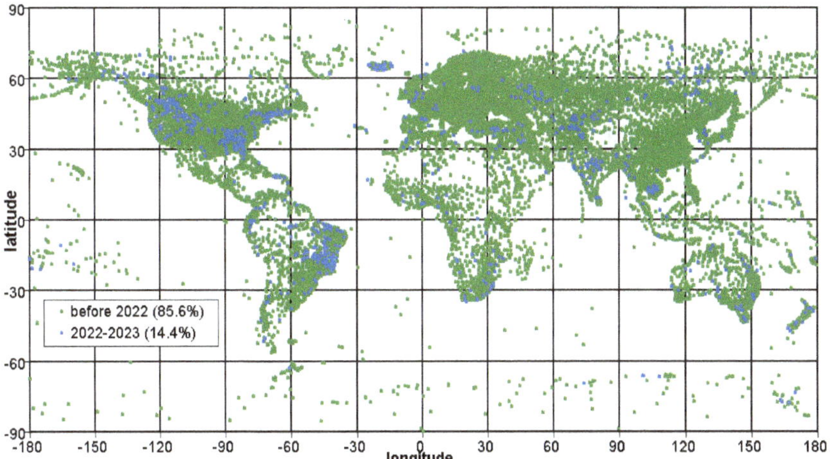

Figure 123. Same Data (GDOS) - Same View – Lows Instead of Highs

There are almost as many global record lows (14.4%) in 2022-2023 as record highs (17.5%) during this same period. What does this say about global warming? This is why the narrative is now called: climate *change*. But can an increase in CO_2 really explain this? Who knows for sure?

There are lots of blue (colder) dots in this figure too (as there were red dots in the preceding one), especially in the Lower 48, where we've already presented the lack of any clear upward or downward trend. These extremes appear to be balancing each other, at least in this region.

83

In this next figure we see the same paint green-the-blue emphasizing the latter as before with the paint green-then-then red.

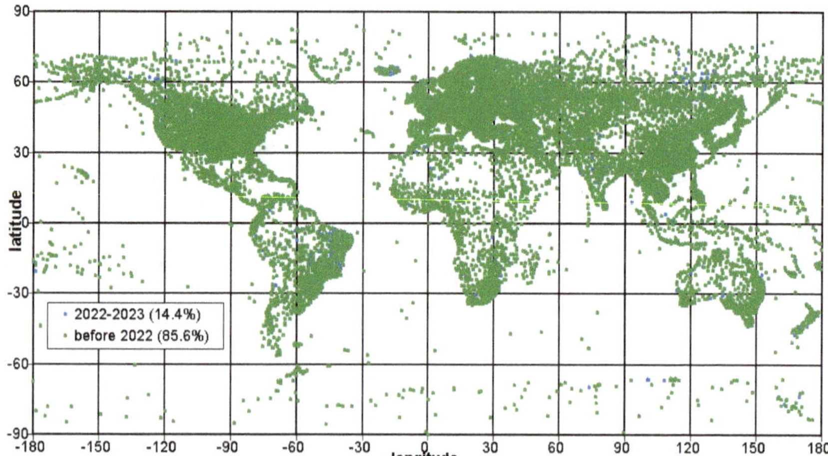

Figure 124. Exact Same Data but Blue before Green

There "appears" to be almost no blue spots in this figure, yet there "appears" to be plenty in the preceding one. Again, beware how data are presented and if there is an *agenda* behind the way in which the data are presented. The two blue or red before green figures might convey that the climate is just the same-old-same-old when it isn't. The climate is changing *and it always has been!*

TP2 (second generation TPLOT) is quite versatile and free at the link below the Preface. It can handle 38 types of files, including: 2D, 3D, and 4D. It can also process data, including: converting several file formats and multi-dimensional interpolation. It contains many examples, which are embedded in the EXE file. In fact, you don't need anything but the EXE file to have it all. It doesn't require any special installation and can simply be deleted should you no longer need it.

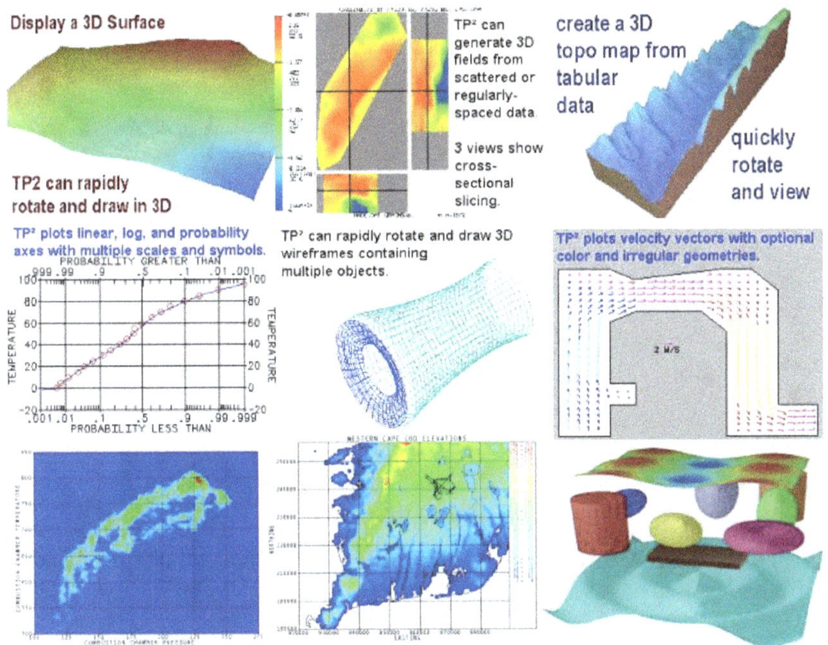

Figure 125. TP2 Samples (all included)

The following file formats are supported:

ext	format	ext	format	ext	format
2DS	2D triangular surface	F3D	Field3D	TB3	volume
2DV	2D finite element	HGL	HPGL	TOP	surface (topo)
3DS	3D Studio	MAP	Field3D	TP2	TP2
3DV	3D finite element	NDE	nodes+elements	TP3	3D function calls
BIN	raw binary image	NM8	Anim8	TRA	triad

BMP	bitmap image	P2D	2D polygons	TRI	triangles
CIR	colored circles	P3D	3D wireframe	V2D	2D vectors
CNT	contours (raw)	PLT	TPLOT	V3D	3D vectors
CON	contours (cooked)	PYR	pyramid	VRM	VirtualRealityModeling
DAT	raw data	RM	Raster MetaFile	WMF	Windows MetaFile
DEM	digital elevation	SPH	colored spheres	WPG	WordPerfectGraphics
DSM	digital sediment	SUR	surface (cooked)	WRL	VirtualRealityMarkup
DXF	drawing	TB2	surface (raw)		

Menu options include:

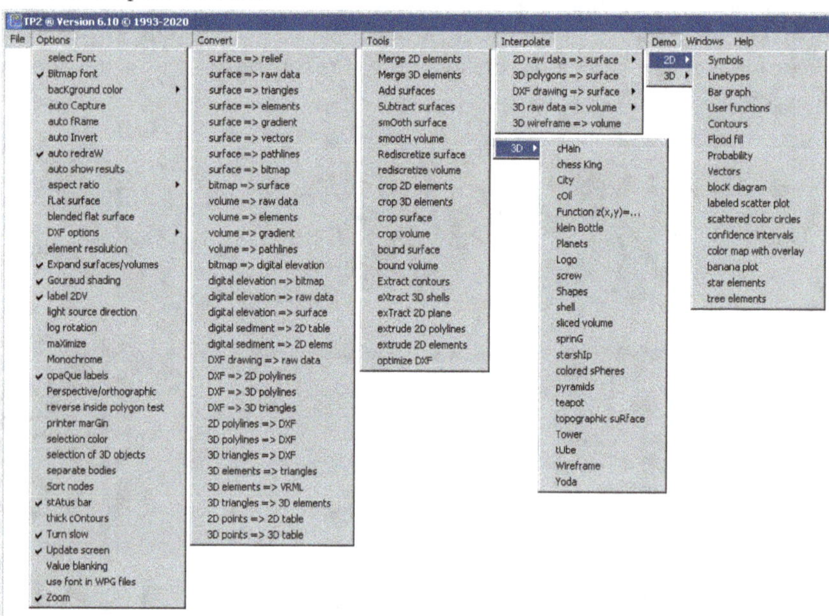

Figure 126. TP2 Options and Features

TP2 will also convert between many file types, which is quite useful when working with 3D models.

Appendix B. Inverse Distance Interpolation

The inverse distance interpolation method is one of the most useful techniques for interpolating data, especially spatially disperse and even more so irregularly spaced. In short, the closer a known point is, the more influence it should have on the local (i.e., interpolated) value. Often a power of 2.5 is applied to the distance. This can be expressed by the following equation.

$$C = \frac{\sum \dfrac{C_I}{R_I^{2.5}}}{\sum \dfrac{1}{R_I^{2.5}}} \tag{B.1}$$

The following code is the simplest implementation of this formula in two dimensions:

```
for(S=C=j=0;j<n;j++)
  {
  d=hypot(X[j]-x,Y[j]-y);
  if(d<DBL_EPSILON)
    d=DBL_EPSILON;
  d=pow(d,2.5);
  s+=1./d;
  c+=C[j]/d;
  }
c/=s;
```

It is necessary to limit the distance so as to not divide by zero. If you're that close, it doesn't matter what the other points are. Depending on how the known points are scattered, unwanted artifacts can arise. For example, if the known points are all clumped together on one side or corner of the domain, this will produce shadows, over-emphasizing the clumped data. These unwanted artifacts can often be eliminated by considering only the closest point in each of four quadrants (or eight octants).

A mistake often made when implementing a quadrant or octant search is to use the a=arctan2(y,x) function and then a series of if(a<M_PI/4.) statements. The arctan function takes far longer to execute than the multiplications, divisions, and even raising distance to a non-integral power. Do NOT use arctan for this purpose. A far easier and vastly faster process is shown in the following code, which can be easily modified for octants:

```
for(i=0;i<4;i++)
  {
  iQ[i]=-1;
  Dq[i]=0.;
  }
for(i=0;i<n;i++)
  {
  dX=x-X[i];
  dY=y-Y[i];
  d=hypot(dX,dY);
  q=0;
  if(dX>0.)
     q|=1;
  if(dY>0.)
     q|=2;
  if(fabs(dX)>fabs(dY))
     q|=4;
  if(d<Dq[q])
     {
     Dq[q]=d;
     iQ[q]=i;
     }
  }
for(C=s=q=0;q<8;q++)
  {
  if(iQ[q]>=0)
    {
    if(Dq[q]>DBL_EPSILON)
       d=pow(Dq[q],2.5);
    else
       d=DBL_EPSILON;
    S+=1./d
    C+=C[iQ[q]]/d;
    }
  }
C/=s;
```

The three simple (and fast) comparisons (i.e., dX>0, dY>0, and |dX|>|dY|) uniquely determine the octant (0-7) by conditionally adding 3 bits (1, 2, and 4), which can only have values 0 through 7. Using the arctan takes at least eight times as long and provides no advantage whatsoever. The code above saves the (double) distance in Dq[8] and (integer) index in iQ[8]. The summation and application of pow(D,2.5) is applied as before. Of course, depending on where you are in the field, some of the octants may be empty, which is why we first fill the array iQ with minus ones.

Spherical Coordinates

Note that the distance between two points on the surface of a sphere (viz., the Earth) is NOT

$$d = \sqrt{\Delta x^2 + \Delta y^2} \qquad \text{(B.2)}$$

on a Mercator map projection. The shortest path between two cities may be over the North Pole.

Figure 127. Distance between Two Points on the Globe

The distance in this case is given by:

$$d = r \times \mathrm{acos}(\sin(\phi_1)\sin(\phi_2) + \cos(\phi_1)\cos(\phi_2)\cos(\lambda_2 - \lambda_1)) \qquad \text{(B.3)}$$

where r is the radius of the Earth, λ is the longitude, and ϕ is the latitude.

The variables are shown in the following figure:

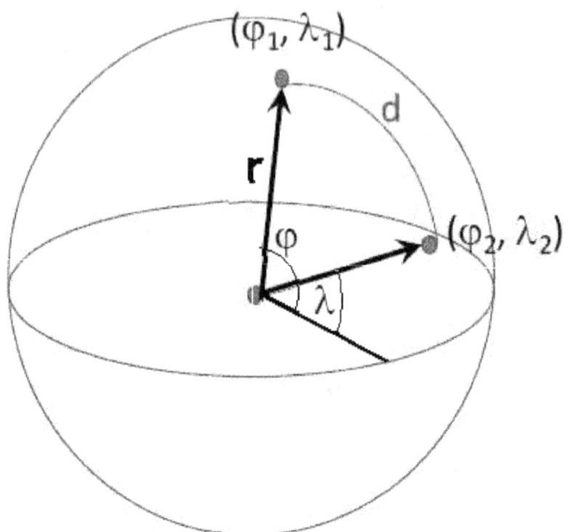

Figure 128. Spherical Coordinate Variables

Appendix C. Kriging

Kriging is a form of Gaussian regression or interpolation used primarily in geostatistics. The original method was developed by Matheron[2] and based on the work of Krige.[3] There are actually a variety of formulas and techniques associated with the term *kriging*, making this designation rather ambiguous. Even a cursory search of the Internet will produce a dozen formulas, many of which (e.g., cos) bear no resemblance to the original concept of Gaussian approximation, which would exhibit an exponential departure outward from known points. Illustrations in one dimension show each data point blending into the next, but this is far removed from the two- and three-dimensional data to which this method is most often applied. The core code is:

```
for(w=d=0;d<Nd;d++)
  {
  Ck[d]=Cd[d];
  for(c=0;c<Nd;c++,w++)
    {
    if(c-d)
      {
      if(dim>2)
        R=hypot3(Xd[c]-Xd[d],Yd[c]-Yd[d],Zd[c]-Zd[d]);
      else
        R=hypot(Xd[c]-Xd[d],Yd[c]-Yd[d]);
      Bd[w]=exp(-R*R/K/K);
      }
    else
      Bd[w]=1.;
    }
  }
for(w=0;w<64;w++)
  {
  for(d=0;d<Nd;d++)
    {
    C=Cd[d];
    for(c=0;c<Nd;c++)
```

---

[2] Georges François Paul Marie Matheron (1930–2000) was French mathematician and civil engineer of mines, known as the founder of geostatistics and a co-founder (together with Jean Serra) of mathematical morphology.

[3] Danie Gerhardus Krige (1919–2013) South African statistician and mining engineer who pioneered the field of geostatistics and was professor at the University of the Witwatersrand.

```c
        if(c-d)
          C-=Ck[d]*Bd[Nd*d+c];

      Ck[d]=fmax(Ck[d]/2.,fmin(2.*Cd[d],(w*Ck[d]+C)/(w+1)))
        ;
        }
    }
for(w=y=0;y<Ny;y++)
    {
    Yi[y]=Ym+y*(Yx-Ym)/(Ny-1);
    for(x=0;x<Nx;x++)
      {
      Xi[x]=Xm+x*(Xx-Xm)/(Nx-1);
      for(C=d=0;d<Nd;d++)
        {
        R=hypot(Xi[x]-Xd[d],Yi[y]-Yd[d]);
        C+=Ck[d]*exp(-R*R/K/K);
        }
      Ci[w++]=C;
        }
    }
```

Appendix D. Map Projections

Map projections attempt to represent a sphere on a flat surface.

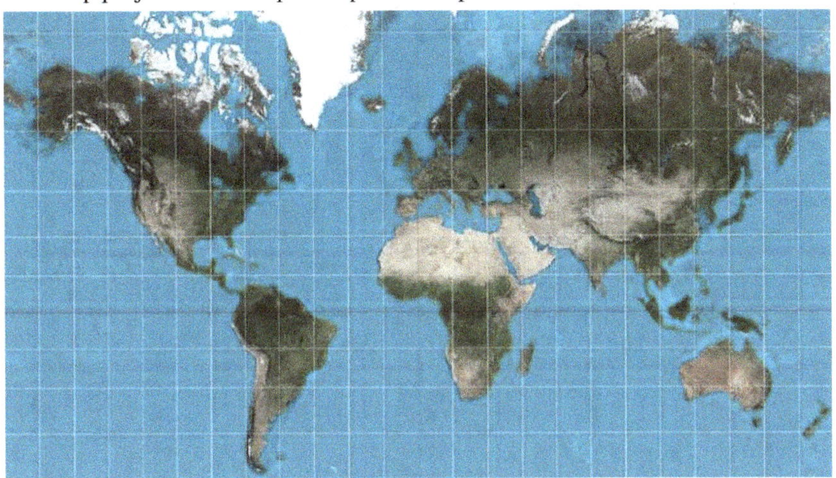

Figure 129. Mercator Map Projection

The Mercator projection has been widely vilified for disproportionately representing various people groups, though it is doubtful that Mercator had such an ulterior motive back in 1569.

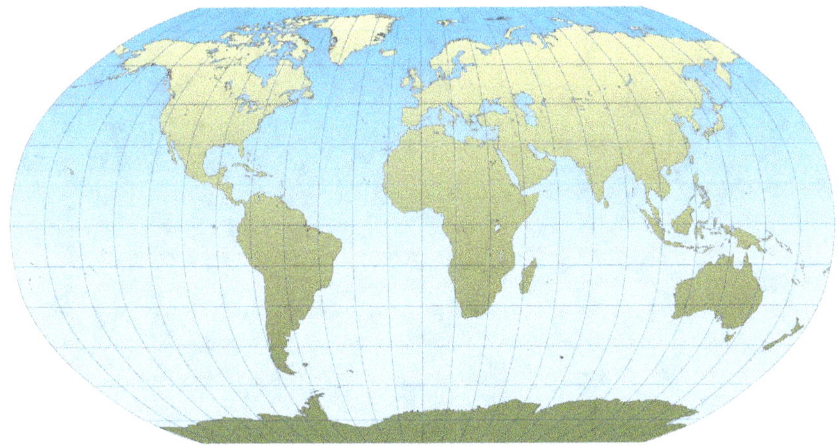

Figure 130. Robinson Map Projection

The Robinson projection is preferred for it's more accurate depiction.

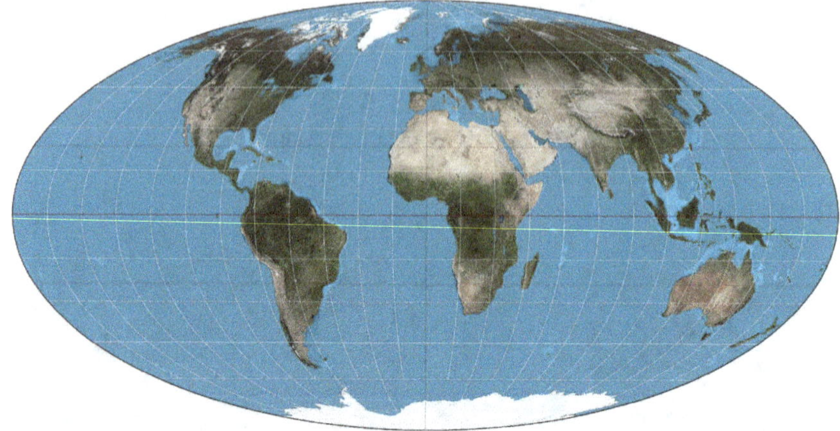

Figure 131. Mollweide Map Projection

The Mercator projection is my personal favorite and can be described geometrically by the following simple equations:

$$x = \frac{2\sqrt{2}}{\pi} \lambda \cos(\theta) \tag{D.1}$$

$$y = \sqrt{2} \sin(\theta) \tag{D.2}$$

where θ is an auxiliary angle defined by:

$$2\theta + \sin(2\theta) = \pi \sin(\phi) \tag{D.3}$$

and λ is the longitude and ϕ is the latitude.

Appendix E. Read Data on the Fly

As we discussed in Chapter, 3 the GSOD collection currently (as of 2023) consists of approximately 877,000 files. We really don't want to extract (untar) and expand (ungzip) all of these and store them in raw form so that they can be read. The best alternative on a Windows™ machine is to process each one as needed, untarring it, ungzipping it, writing it, reading it, and deleting it. There are never more than 2 extra files: the .gz (zipped) and .op (unzipped) one. To accomplish this, we get the C source code off the GNU website, which comes with the following credits:

> Copyright © 1992-1993 Jean-loup Gailly The unzip code was written and put in the public domain by Mark Adler. Portions of the lzw code are derived from the public domain 'compress' written by Spencer Thomas, Joe Orost, James Woods, Jim McKie, Steve Davies, Ken Turkowski, Dave Mack and Peter Jannesen.

We comment out the main program and compile it into a library providing the function unzip(), which we call from inside the code analyzing the data. The whole code to accomplish the in-program part is listed here:

```c
struct{name1[100];mode[8],owner[8],group1[8],fsize[12],
    time[12],checksum[8],flag,name2[100],ustar[6],
    version[2],user[32],group2[32],major[8],minor[8],
    name3[155],padding[12];}header;
int ReadTemperatures(int year)
  {
  char archive[FILENAME_MAX],unzipped[21],zipped[21];
  char bufr[512],*ptr,USAF[]="123456",WBAN[]="12345",
    YEAR[5]="1930";
  int aday,asize,da,data,fsize,i,jday,l,last,mo,s,yr;
  double temp,usaf,wban,yyyymmdd;
  FILE*Farc,*Finp,*Fout;
  STATION station;
  for(s=0;s<stations;s++)
    for(aday=0;aday<366;aday++)
      Station[s].temp[aday]=-999.;
  last=-1;
  sprintf(archive,"%s\\gsod_%i.tar",data_path,year);
  printf("%s\n",archive);
  if((Farc=fopen(archive,"rb"))==NULL)
    return(last);
  asize=_filelength(_fileno(Farc));
  data=0;
```

```c
while(fread(&header,1,sizeof(header),Farc)==
  sizeof(header))
  {
  if(_memicmp(header.ustar,"ustar",5))
    continue;
  if(header.flag!='0')
    continue;
  for(l=1,fsize=i=0;i<11;i++,l*=8)
    fsize+=l*(int)(header.fsize[10-i]-'0');
  if(asize-ftell(Farc)<512*((fsize+511)/512))
    break;
  if((ptr=strrchr(header.name1,'/'))!=NULL)
    ptr++;
  else
    ptr=header.name1;
  memcpy(USAF,ptr,6);
  if(strspn(USAF,"0123456789")<6)
    {
    fseek(Finp,512*((fsize+511)/512),SEEK_CUR);
    continue;
    }
  if(ptr[6]!='-')
    {
    fseek(Finp,512*((fsize+511)/512),SEEK_CUR);
    continue;
    }
  memcpy(WBAN,ptr+7,5);
  if(strspn(WBAN,"0123456789")<5)
    {
    fseek(Finp,512*((fsize+511)/512),SEEK_CUR);
    continue;
    }
  if(ptr[12]!='-')
    {
    fseek(Finp,512*((fsize+511)/512),SEEK_CUR);
    continue;
    }
  memcpy(YEAR,ptr+13,4);
  if(strspn(YEAR,"0123456789")<4)
    {
    fseek(Finp,512*((fsize+511)/512),SEEK_CUR);
    continue;
    }
  if(atoi(YEAR)!=year)
    {
    fseek(Finp,512*((fsize+511)/512),SEEK_CUR);
    continue;
    }
  sprintf(zipped,"%s-%s-%i.gz",USAF,WBAN,year);
```

```c
printf("\r%s",zipped);
if((Fout=fopen(zipped,"wb"))==NULL)
  Abort(__LINE__,"can't create extract file");
while(fsize>0)
  {
  if((l=fread(bufr,1,512,Farc))!=512)
    Abort(__LINE__,"an error occurred while
        reading archive\n512 bytes expected %i
        bytes read",l);
  if((l=fwrite(bufr,1,min(512,fsize),Fout))
      !=min(512,fsize))
    Abort(__LINE__,"an error occurred while
        writing file\n%i bytes expected %i bytes
        written",min(512,fsize),l);
  fsize-=min(512,fsize);
  }
fclose(Fout);
if((Finp=fopen(zipped,"rb"))==NULL)
  Abort(__LINE__,"can't open extract file");
ifd=_fileno(Finp);
ifile_size=_filelength(ifd);
sprintf(unzipped,"%s-%s-%i.op",USAF,WBAN,year);
if((Fout=fopen(unzipped,"wb"))==NULL)
  Abort(__LINE__,"can't create decompressed file");
ofd=_fileno(Fout);
decompress=1;
quiet=1;
verbose=0;
no_name=1;
no_time=1;
time_stamp=0;
clear_bufs();
method=get_method(ifd);
if(method!=DEFLATED)
  Abort(__LINE__,"unsupported compression method");
if(unzip(ifd,ofd)!=OK)
  Abort(__LINE__,"decompression failed");
fclose(Fout);
fclose(Finp);
remove(zipped);
if((Finp=fopen(unzipped,"rt"))==NULL)
  Abort(__LINE__,"can't open decompressed file");
while(fgets(bufr,sizeof(bufr),Finp))
  {
  if(!strchr(bufr,'\n'))
    break;
  if(sscanf(bufr,"%lf %lf %lf
%lf",&usaf,&wban,&yyyymmdd,&temp)!=4)
    continue;
```

```c
      station.usaf=nint(usaf);
      station.wban=nint(wban);
      s=GetStation(&station);
      if(s<0||s>=stations)
         continue;
      i=nint(yyyymmdd);
      yr=i/10000;
      i-=yr*10000;
      mo=i/100;
      i-=mo*100;
      da=i;
      if(yr!=year)
         continue;
      jday=Julian(yr,mo,da);
      aday=jday-Julian(yr,1,1);
      last=max(last,jday);
      Station[s].temp[aday]=temp;
      data++;
      }
   fclose(Finp);
   remove(unzipped);
   }
fclose(Farc);
printf("\r%i data points found\n",data);
YearMonthDay(last,&yr,&mo,&da);
printf("last date was %i/%i/%i\n",mo,da,yr);
return(last);
}
```

Appendix F. Tessellations of a Sphere

The quickest way to break a sphere down into individual triangular elements is tessellation. We begin with a cube and split each side over-and-over again until the grid is fine enough to meet our needs.

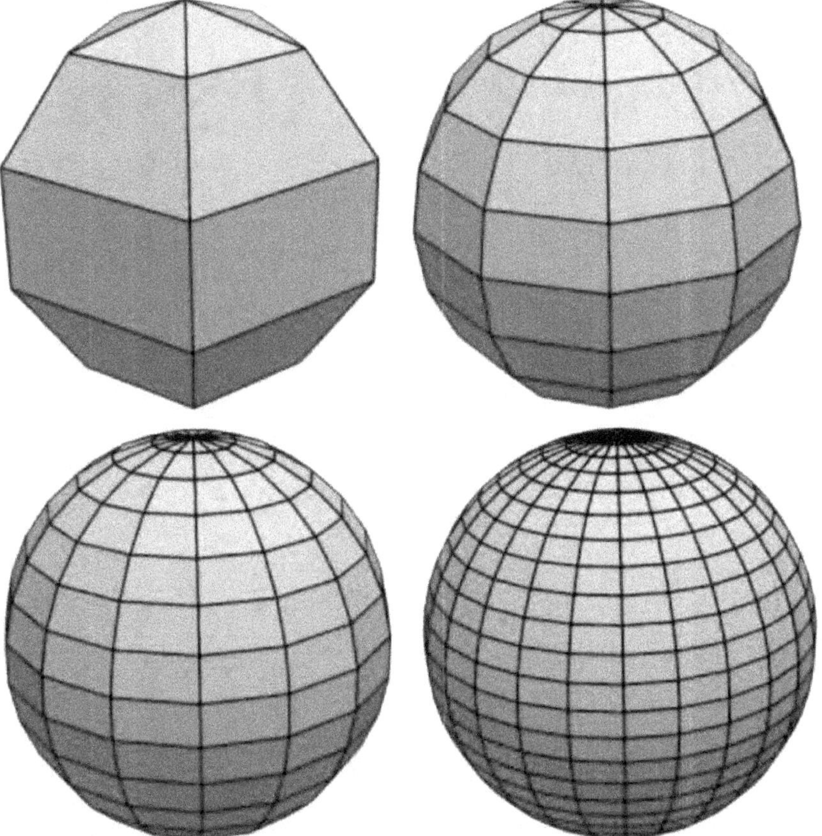

Figure 132. Sequential Tessellations of a Sphere

There are many algorithms available on the Web. The following one is attributed to Jon Leech 3/24/89:

```
          1
         /\
        /  \
       /    \
    b/______\c
     /\      /\
    /  \    /  \
   /____\/____\
  0      a      2
```

```
make new points
  a=(0+2)/2
  b=(0+1)/2
  c=(1+2)/2
normalize a,b,c
construct new triangles
  [0,b,a]
  [b,1,c]
  [a,b,c]
  [a,c,2]
```

```c
for(level=1;level<maxlevels;level++)
  {
  new=(OBJECT*)malloc(sizeof(OBJECT));
  new->npoly=old->npoly*4;
  new->poly=malloc(new->npoly*sizeof(TRIANGLE));
    for(i=0;i<old->npoly;i++)
    {
    TRIANGLE*oldt=&old->poly[i];
    TRIANGLE*newt=&new->poly[i*4];
    POINT a,b,c;
    a=*Normalize(Midpoint(&oldt->pt[0],&oldt->pt[2]));
    b=*Normalize(Midpoint(&oldt->pt[0],&oldt->pt[1]));
    c=*Normalize(Midpoint(&oldt->pt[1],&oldt->pt[2]));
    newt->pt[0]=oldt->pt[0];
    newt->pt[1]=b;
    newt->pt[2]=a;
    newt++;
    newt->pt[0]=b;
    newt->pt[1]=oldt->pt[1];
    newt->pt[2]=c;
    newt++;
    newt->pt[0]=a;
    newt->pt[1]=b;
    newt->pt[2]=c;
    newt++;
    newt->pt[0]=a;
    newt->pt[1]=c;
    newt->pt[2]=oldt->pt[2];
    }
  if(level>1)
    {
    free(old->poly);
    free(old);
    }
  old=new;
  }
```

also by D. James Benton

3D Articulation: Using OpenGL, ISBN-9798596362480, Amazon, 2021 (book 3 in the 3D series).

3D Models in Motion Using OpenGL, ISBN-9798652987701, Amazon, 2020 (book 2 in the 3D series.

3D Rendering in Windows: How to display three-dimensional objects in Windows with and without OpenGL, ISBN-9781520339610, Amazon, 2016 (book 1 in the 3D series).

A Synergy of Short Stories: The whole may be greater than the sum of the parts, ISBN-9781520340319, Amazon, 2016.

Azeotropes: Behavior and Application, ISBN-9798609748997, Amazon, 2020.

bat-Elohim: Book 3 in the Little Star Trilogy, ISBN-9781686148682, Amazon, 2019.

Boilers: Performance and Testing, ISBN: 9798789062517, Amazon 2021.

Combined 3D Rendering Series: 3D Rendering in Windows®, 3D Models in Motion, and 3D Articulation, ISBN-9798484417032, Amazon, 2021.

Complex Variables: Practical Applications, ISBN-9781794250437, Amazon, 2019.

Compression & Encryption: Algorithms & Software, ISBN-9781081008826, Amazon, 2019.

Computational Fluid Dynamics: an Overview of Methods, ISBN-9781672393775, Amazon, 2019.

Computer Simulation of Power Systems: Programming Strategies and Practical Examples, ISBN-9781696218184, Amazon, 2019.

Contaminant Transport: A Numerical Approach, ISBN-9798461733216, Amazon, 2021.

CPUnleashed! Tapping Processor Speed, ISBN-9798421420361, Amazon, 2022.

Curve-Fitting: The Science and Art of Approximation, ISBN-9781520339542, Amazon, 2016.

Death by Tie: It was the best of ties. It was the worst of ties. It's what got him killed., ISBN-9798398745931, Amazon, 2023.

Differential Equations: Numerical Methods for Solving, ISBN-9781983004162, Amazon, 2018.

Equations of State: A Graphical Comparison, ISBN-9798843139520, Amazon, 2022.

Evaporative Cooling: The Science of Beating the Heat, ISBN-9781520913346, Amazon, 2017.

Forecasting: Extrapolation and Projection, ISBN-9798394019494, Amazon 2023.

Heat Engines: Thermodynamics, Cycles, & Performance Curves, ISBN-9798486886836, Amazon, 2021.

Heat Exchangers: Performance Prediction & Evaluation, ISBN-9781973589327, Amazon, 2017.

Heat Recovery Steam Generators: Thermal Design and Testing, ISBN-9781691029365, Amazon, 2019.

Heat Transfer: Heat Exchangers, Heat Recovery Steam Generators, & Cooling Towers, ISBN-9798487417831, Amazon, 2021.

Heat Transfer Examples: Practical Problems Solved, ISBN-9798390610763, Amazon, 2023.

The Kick-Start Murders: Visualize revenge, ISBN-9798759083375, Amazon, 2021.

Jamie2: Innocence is easily lost and cannot be restored, ISBN-9781520339375, Amazon, 2016-18.

Kyle Cooper Mysteries: Kick Start, Monte Carlo, and Waterfront Murders, ISBN-9798829365943, Amazon, 2022.

The Last Seraph: Sequel to Little Star, ISBN-9781726802253, Amazon, 2018.

Little Star: God doesn't do things the way we expect Him to. He's better than that! ISBN-9781520338903, Amazon, 2015-17.

Living Math: Seeing mathematics in every day life (and appreciating it more too), ISBN-9781520336992, Amazon, 2016.

Lost Cause: If only history could be changed..., ISBN-9781521173770, Amazon, 2017.

Mass Transfer: Diffusion & Convection, ISBN-9798702403106, Amazon, 2021.

Mill Town Destiny: The Hand of Providence brought them together to rescue the mill, the town, and each other, ISBN-9781520864679, Amazon, 2017.

Monte Carlo Murders: Who Killed Who and Why, ISBN-9798829341848, Amazon, 2022.

Monte Carlo Simulation: The Art of Random Process Characterization, ISBN-9781980577874, Amazon, 2018.

Nonlinear Equations: Numerical Methods for Solving, ISBN-9781717767318, Amazon, 2018.

Numerical Calculus: Differentiation and Integration, ISBN-9781980680901, Amazon, 2018.

Numerical Methods: Nonlinear Equations, Numerical Calculus, & Differential Equations, ISBN-9798486246845, Amazon, 2021.

Orthogonal Functions: The Many Uses of, ISBN-9781719876162, Amazon, 2018.

Overwhelming Evidence: A Pilgrimage, ISBN-9798515642211, Amazon, 2021.

Particle Tracking: Computational Strategies and Diverse Examples, ISBN-9781692512651, Amazon, 2019.

Plumes: Delineation & Transport, ISBN-9781702292771, Amazon, 2019.

Power Plant Performance Curves: for Testing and Dispatch, ISBN-9798640192698, Amazon, 2020.

Practical Linear Algebra: Principles & Software, ISBN-9798860910584, Amazon, 2023.

Props, Fans, & Pumps: Design & Performance, ISBN-9798645391195, Amazon, 2020.

Remediation: Contaminant Transport, Particle Tracking, & Plumes, ISBN-9798485651190, Amazon, 2021.

ROFL: Rolling on the Floor Laughing, ISBN-9781973300007, Amazon, 2017.

Seminole Rain: You don't choose destiny. It chooses you, ISBN-9798668502196, Amazon, 2020.

Septillionth: 1 in 10^{24}, ISBN-9798410762472, Amazon, 2022.

Software Development: Targeted Applications, ISBN-9798850653989, Amazon, 2023.

Software Recipes: Proven Tools, ISBN-9798815229556, Amazon, 2022.

Steam 2020: to 150 GPa and 6000 K, ISBN-9798634643830, Amazon, 2020.

Thermochemical Reactions: Numerical Solutions, ISBN-9781073417872, Amazon, 2019.

Thermodynamic and Transport Properties of Fluids, ISBN-9781092120845, Amazon, 2019.

Thermodynamic Cycles: Effective Modeling Strategies for Software Development, ISBN-9781070934372, Amazon, 2019.

Thermodynamics - Theory & Practice: The science of energy and power, ISBN-9781520339795, Amazon, 2016.

Version-Independent Programming: Code Development Guidelines for the Windows® Operating System, ISBN-9781520339146, Amazon, 2016.

The Waterfront Murders: As you sow, so shall you reap, ISBN-9798611314500, Amazon, 2020.